NEW BEGINNINGS

STEP INTO THE LIFE
YOU WERE CREATED TO LIVE

ANTHONY FONTE

ISBN: 978-0-692-85505-8

Printed in the United States of America.

THE STORY
BEHIND THE FRONT COVER PHOTO

I want to take a moment and share the inspiration behind the front cover photo. The photo was actually inspired by my daughter, Kailee. One evening, I was getting some work done and Kailee was in her room playing with her dolls. She had been playing in her room for quite some time, when suddenly she came out of the room and said to me, "Daddy, I know what the cover of your book should be." I immediately stopped what I was doing to listen to her, because it came out of nowhere. Something obviously inspired her, so I was listening intently. I said to her, "What do you think it should be?" She responds, "I think it should be a picture with a sunset, and a person standing in a field with their arms up in victory." I replied, "I like that, but how about something better? Instead of it being a sunset, we can make it a sunrise, and instead of a person in the field, it's you and me standing in a field looking at the sunrise because a sunrise represents a new beginning." With that, the photo was brought to life. This isn't just a new beginning for me. It's a new beginning for Kailee as well, so it's important to me that her voice be heard. With something bigger guiding that inspiration, this was my way of letting her voice be heard.

This book is dedicated to:

Jennifer Leigh Fonte

and

Donna Marie Fonte

We miss and love you very much

CONTENTS

INTRODUCTION 1

CHAPTER 1. YOU ARE NOT DEFINED BY YOUR PAST . . . 19

CHAPTER 2. FORGIVENESS 27

CHAPTER 3. HAPPINESS COMES FROM WITHIN 35

CHAPTER 4. BEING CONTENT WHERE YOU ARE 41

CHAPTER 5. BOASTING IN YOUR WEAKNESSES 49

CHAPTER 6. YOU CAN'T DO IT ALONE 57

CHAPTER 7. LETTING GO OF WHAT YOU CAN'T CONTROL . 65

CHAPTER 8. WHAT YOU FOCUS ON GROWS 75

CHAPTER 9. LIVE IN THE MOMENT 83

CHAPTER 10. WALKING THROUGH GRIEF 91

FINAL THOUGHTS 101

ABOUT THE AUTHOR 103

INTRODUCTION

This book is dedicated to the person that has experienced a life changing event and is having a hard time moving forward. That event can be death, divorce, loss of a dream, or loss of a goal. It can be loss of passion, loss of self, loss of intimacy in marriage, or an event from childhood that still has a stranglehold on you today. It does not matter what you have experienced. If you are stuck or lost, feeling overwhelmed, anxious, sad, frustrated, angry, bitter, fearful, or any number of emotions that could be holding you back, then this book is for you.

This book is dedicated to the person that knows the kind of life they deserve. A life full of happiness and joy. A life full of significance, purpose, and meaning. A life filled with passion and living in that passion every single day. A life filled with empowering relationships and marriages. A life that is balanced in all areas. A life that when you imagine, it instantly brings a smile to your face and you feel the weight of all your past negative experiences disappear.

This book is dedicated to the person that has been beaten down by life over and over again and has lost hope and faith. The person that has done well, but feels like something is missing from their life, or has hit a block and is unable to go to the next level. The person that says, "There has to be more to life than this," or "I know I was made for more." The person that is sick and tired of being sick and tired. The person that is saying, "Something has to give," or "what do I do now?" The person that is trying to find who they are, or trying to redefine who they are. The list goes on and on, but I think you get the point. If you have experienced something in your life and feel lost or stuck in any way, then this book is for you.

The pages within have so much meaning to me and my hope is that by the time you have finished reading this book the pages have meaning to you as well. Even if only one statement helps you, then this book has done its job.

I have used the lessons in this book and continue to use them to this day, to grow and create positive changes in my life. I heard it once said that the day we stop growing and learning is the day we die. That statement is empowering to me because it is very true, especially if we are wanting change in our lives. We cannot continue to do the same things over and over and expect different results. That, my friends, is the definition of insanity. When it comes to life changing events, I have found that is what tends to happen. We continue doing the same things over and over. We continue in the same limiting thought patterns that keep holding us back. We continue to blame others and become bitter or angry. We become sad or depressed. We tend to give up and accept our current situation, thinking there is no way out and this is the life we are meant to have. We get stuck in these patterns often times, by no fault of our own as we are not aware of the conditioning of our past, our behaviors, and our actions. If we want change in our lives, we have to take responsibility for ourselves. Although we cannot control circumstances outside of us, we are still responsible for how we react to a given situation. The Bible talks about the fruit of the spirit. Part of the fruit is self-control. Not control of anything else, but the control of one's self.

I want you to know that although your journey is specific to you, you are not alone while you walk this path. There have been countless people that have been exactly where you are today. I have been through just about every loss you can imagine and I want you to know that although it may seem unbearable, you will make it through, emerging as a much stronger, amazing, version of the real you. I promise.

Something else that I can promise you is that I will be completely vulnerable and transparent. Some think that being vulnerable and transparent is a sign of weakness, allowing people to judge you and look down on you. I have found in my own experience that the exact opposite is true. My hope, by sharing my story and lessons I've learned, is that it will reach the right person, so that they may feel inspired and empowered to break free, to have the life they were created for. My hope is that you find your passion and fulfill your purpose. My hope is that you take back control of your life and find who you were created to be. If this book helps just one person, then my purpose will be fulfilled. We are all here to help each other and I believe that the storms we go through can be used to teach us something, to make good out of the bad. It's all about the perspective we choose to view our struggles.

THE BEGINNING YEARS

To really grasp how my story unfolds, I need to first take you back to the beginning. The past five years have been the bulk of my learning, but it all began when I was a young boy.

I come from a strict Italian background. My dad is full blooded Italian and was raised in a very strict and unpleasant environment. Anger, a controlling nature, and emotional belittling appeared to be norm in the home from what I have gathered through stories told by my parents, as well as my aunt and uncles who grew up in the house. My dad is the oldest of five so he received the brunt of it. Since that is all my dad knew, he then passed it on to my brother and I. It was not easy growing up with my dad. My mom, on the other hand, was very loving, although she had her moments as most moms do. As parents (and humans) we stumble from time to time. Mom was the encourager and I am not ashamed to admit that I was kind of a momma's boy.

Although my mom could be hard on us at times, it was nothing compared to my dad. My brother and I grew up not knowing if our dad really loved us, or if he even wanted us around. Have you ever been in a situation where you felt unimportant in the eyes of someone you really looked up to? Have you wanted someone to be so proud of you, but knew that nothing you ever did could make that a reality? Have you ever felt that it did not matter whether you existed or not?

That is how I felt growing up with my dad. He was unhappy most of the time, and that unhappiness manifested into anger. He was consumed by anger on the inside, as was apparent in his facial expressions, his demeanor, his behaviors, and especially with the way he spoke to us. The brief moments that I remember seeing him remotely happy were when he was out somewhere with a buddy or family, at home with some friends, or out fishing with us. There were more happy moments in his life, I am sure, but we rarely saw them.

Often times, out of anger, he would call us "stupid" and tell us that we would never amount to anything. To this day, I do not like the word, "stupid." Up until the recent past, I would get very upset if someone called me stupid, even if they were only joking. I have since gained the wisdom that a word or experience only has personal meaning if we allow it to. I changed the meaning of the word stupid so that I do not personally attach myself or my childhood experiences to it. I still do not prefer to use the word, but it no longer affects me as it once did. Idiot, dumb, and dumbass are some close alternatives that I prefer not to use as well. My dad would use those words also, just not as often as stupid, so the emotional attachment was not as great as it was with stupid.

In school, there began a struggle between doing well academically and the anger that was consuming me. I was constantly hearing my dad's voice in the back of my head reminding me that I was stupid and wouldn't amount to anything. This debilitating struggle began to manifest itself in my daily behavior. My sophomore year was probably my worst year. I lashed out at teachers and turned my back on authority altogether. I even threw a desk once after getting so angry at my teacher for keeping me after class and giving me detention. I felt as if she was picking on me and I lashed out against her. It seemed like every other week I was in in school suspension. I even got suspended for stabbing a kid with a pen, because he would not stop staring at me. Pretty bad, right? If I had the opportunity, I would ask that person for forgiveness. I can only imagine the pain I caused him physically and emotionally. That being said, most of the time you couldn't even tell that I was so angry as I was always telling jokes, being crazy, and making others laugh. Being funny was a defense mechanism to hide my own pain.

I never wanted others to feel the inner turmoil I was feeling.

I wanted to make my dad proud. Going through school, I would find myself trying to prove that I was not stupid and that I could accomplish great things. Surprisingly I did well in school despite getting in trouble quite often. Between the fighting, causing distractions, and other shenanigans, I still managed to get good grades.

At the time, graduating high school was the biggest accomplishment for me and I was proud of my achievement. I was the only one that graduated high school in my family, so I thought my dad would be proud of me as well. Graduation day came but my dad didn't show up. I was absolutely crushed. I played it off and just kept saying, "I'm fine," and "it's his loss for not being there," but subconsciously, my dad not being there caused a deep wound that would not present itself until later. When my dad did not show, it strengthened the perception I had of him that he did not love me and was not proud of me, no matter what I did.

Let me make clear that I am not sharing this story about my dad to bash him. That is not the case at all. The purpose here is to let you envision where my struggles ultimately began. I have learned that for some people, they do not know how to love, or they have a very hard time expressing love. The love is there, they just don't know how to show it. My dad is one of those people. He was the oldest of five and was not really shown what love should be. He was taught "tough love," so that is all he knew. Up until a few years ago, I could only remember my dad saying "I love you" a handful of times. Even then, you could tell it was hard for him to do. I used to long for him to show me that he loved me and that he was proud of me. I finally realized that he just does not know how and I have accepted it. I know he loves me, just in his own way.

Now, the joke is to sneak a hug in on him when he does not expect it just to get a rise out of him. My brother and I will take turns distracting him or sneaking up on him and wrapping our arms around him to give him a hug. We have to be sure to secure his arms or he will hit us. It is extremely funny to see his response and it's absolutely worth it every time. This is only possible now that we have changed our perception and no longer need our dad to show us love. My dad has made some changes as well, and although he does not know how to express it, I know he wishes he could have changed things from the past. We all do. Although we cannot change the past, we can learn from it and make changes that affect today, and our future.

THE MIDDLE YEARS

Immediately after graduation, I joined the United States Air Force. I was scheduled to leave in April of 1994. In the meantime, I would work here and there, jumping from job to job. I began to get bored, and when an 18-year-old gets bored, they often end up making bad decisions. I was no exception. I got in trouble for property damage which landed me in some pretty serious trouble. I had to go to court and find an attorney that would help me. I found one and he advised that I get a document stating my enlistment in the military. I did not know it at the time, but that document ended up being my "Get out of jail free" card. The judge felt that going into the military would be the best thing for me and dropped the charges. I was extremely grateful and relieved.

Some of the people I was hanging around were not the greatest influence and thankfully I could finally see that. I was wise enough to know I was going to go make some more bad decisions if I continued the same path, so I asked my recruiter if he could find me something sooner than April as I wanted to get out of town and on to a fresh start. At 8 AM on January 5, 1994, I got the call from my recruiter. He asked me if I was awake. I replied, "Yes." He said, "Are you sure?" I again replied, "Yes." He said, "Well, if you're not, you will be after I tell you the news I have for you." He proceeded to tell me that he found a career opportunity for me as a Munitions Systems Specialist that I would be pretty excited about. I was to leave the next day and had to be at the federal building in Saint Louis that evening. Needless to say, I was definitely awake at that point. I had just a few hours to say goodbye to my friends, my family, and pack a small bag, and get my butt downtown per military regulation so that I would prepared to leave for basic training. The next day I was sworn in and off to San Antonio, TX for basic training.

I spent six weeks in basic training with limited access to my family, and the civilian world. After basic training I was immediately sent to Denver for two months of extensive training as a Munitions Systems Specialist. I had some anger issues and problems with authority during my career training, but overall, I did well. After basic training and my career training were complete, I was stationed in South Carolina where I completed most of my four year enlistment. Shortly after I arrived in South Carolina, I began to talk to my ex-girlfriend from Saint Louis again. Our relationship was always rocky and was constantly on again, off again. This time instead of getting back together to date, we made the decision to get married and she would move down to South Carolina with me.

We got married right before my 19th birthday. Looking back, I was unsure of why I really married this person. As I stated, we did not have the greatest relationship when we were dating and all the signs showed that we should not have gotten married. I will share later on what I believe led me to getting married, but at the time, I thought I was in love. That being said, I got a beautiful son and daughter out of it. The marriage was a roller coaster which added stress and increased my anger over time.

The stress and anger from my marriage overwhelmed me to the point that it began spilling out into my work and friendships. I would lash out at friends over the tiniest things. They would get mad at first but empathized with my situation and quickly let it go. The pain got to the point where I became numb and just did not care anymore. I shut down and didn't let anyone in. I felt alone and was convinced that I had to deal with my struggles on my own. After all, that is how I was taught. At one point, I lost my security clearance and had to work at the commander's office for fear of hurting other people. My job involved building bombs and missiles and handling many other munitions, so I could understand the concern. I eventually got my clearance back, but it took a long time and a whole lot of hard work.

Instead of dealing with the issues, I turned to drinking to drown out the pain. When we run from our problems instead of facing them, it typically does not end well. Unfortunately, when we run from our problems, they never go away. They will still be there when the alcohol wears off and we're forced to return to reality. More often than not, when we run, our problems tend to get worse. In my case, I got arrested twice in one week which almost caused me to get dishonorably discharged. I luckily did not get kicked out and quit drinking for 9 months. I was still angry and bitter on the inside, but tried to squash it down in front of other people. Occasionally, the inner turmoil would come out and I would eventually start lashing out again.

After months of heartache and anger, my wife and I got separated for the last time and the divorce was filed. In the middle of the divorce, I was sent overseas to Qatar. I actually volunteered to go, because I wanted to escape from everything. While over there I had a close call with death when a supervisor accidentally armed a fuse in one of the bombs we were building. When I tell this story, people ask if the bomb ever exploded. I reply with, "No, I actually died and you are talking to my ghost?" Then I laugh. The only thing that prevented that bomb from exploding was a safety mechanism in the fuse. Had there been a short in the fuse, I would not be here. That event made me think about all the things we take for granted and rethink my life. However, that gratitude did not last as it wasn't long before the old patterns began to resurface.

After four months, I returned from Qatar to visit family in Saint Louis. While at my mom's, she handed me a letter and advised that I may want to sit down to read it. I blew it off, but took the letter anyway. The first sentence I read included the phrase "by the way, my daughter is yours." I was shocked. My daughter was almost 6 when I received that letter. I had a million different thoughts going through my head and for a while I just sat there looking at the letter in disbelief. Was I dreaming? Was this a joke? If it was a joke, it sure wasn't funny! I decided do the right thing so I reached out to her mother to let her know that I wanted to step up as her father. I had a paternity test which proved that I was indeed the father. I was excited to get to know her, but shortly after the results were in and court was finalized, her mother stopped returning my calls and emails. She lived in another state and financially, I was not capable to go out there. I made several attempts in the courts to see her with no prevail. I felt that I had done everything that I could do, so I gave up at that time.

My biggest regret here is whether or not I fought hard enough to see her. I know I cannot change the past and I have learned to let it go, but for a long time that regret haunted me. I later learned that I could not change it, so I needed to stop beating myself up over it. I was eventually able to overcome the regret and let it go.

In January 1998, I was honorably discharged from the military. After the military, I decided I wanted to be my own boss and thought real estate would be the greatest opportunity, so I decided to get my license. However, as with any business, it's hard to keep going if you don't have money on reserve to keep up with the costs, so that was short-lived. I had to accept a job as an assistant manager in retail to bring in some income in order to support my kids that I did have joint custody of. I kept telling myself I would continue doing real estate on a part-time basis until I could go full-time again, but I got comfortable working a 9-5 job and never followed through. I continued to switch jobs in pursuit of making enough income to take care of my kids as well as all of my needs. Many of the jobs I accepted did not pay enough to take care of two kids for the two weeks that I had them so I would jump around to find something that seemed to have more opportunities. I would also take on several risks as an entrepreneur which did not pan out and further hurt my financial situation. As a way to offset the financial losses, I would continue to jump from career to career that offered more money and more reward. However, the enthusiasm would soon wear off and I would be unhappy again.

After years of this, I decided to go to school and get a degree. I loved numbers and math which led me to accounting. In the beginning, I excelled. I was consistently getting A's and B's and loving it. However, after a few semesters, my energy and focus changed once again. I began to self-sabotage my efforts, but could not understand why. I began to get anxious and would burst out in uncontrollable raging fits. I damaged many relationships as a result of my behavior. After some time, I realized I had a problem and did not like the way I was feeling, so I went to see a doctor and shared my situation, which was extremely hard for me to do. I had to share my weakness, and felt that I was less of a man for asking for help. I was always taught to deal with my own problems and not to seek help from outside. In our family, men didn't seek help, and if they did, that was a sign of weakness. After nervously sharing my situation with the doctor, I found out that I suffered from depression, but did not understand why I was depressed. After about six months, it was clear why! I was still deeply scarred by my dad's refusal to come to my high school graduation and feared that the pattern would continue when I graduated college.

I was on medicine for two years and for that two years I never got better, I was still depressed. As a matter of fact, my situation got worse. I began drinking heavily again and destroyed even more relationships. It was at this point that I learned medicine only masks the symptoms, it doesn't fix the root of the problem. Although medicine may be necessary to aid someone so they can get to a healing point, unless you get to the root cause, the problem will never go away. After approximately one year of being on the medicine, I had enough. I declared that depression was not going to win. That moment changed something inside of me. Within a year, I was off my medicine and doing better even though I still had some unresolved issues that would resurface later on in my life

After 5 years, I finally graduated with my bachelor's degree in Accounting and landed a great job making more money than I have ever made, and yet I still was not fulfilled. Again, I began searching for more opportunities to make more money, most of them ending badly. Of course, I also wanted to "keep up with the Joneses" which landed me in bankruptcy. You may have noticed there seems to be a pattern that keeps resurfacing here that will be revealed as the chapters in this book unfold.

After approximately 2 years, I realized that accounting wasn't the best fit for me, so I decided to jump into a career that I thought would be more rewarding, as it would be helping people and had the potential to make more money. I decided to become a financial advisor. I started part-time for about a year before going full-time. Unfortunately, this also happened to be during a recession and the housing market crash. I know, what you're thinking. You're thinking, "What a great time to go full-time in the financial industry, Einstein!" Need I remind you that many of my decisions were based irrationally on the lack of being fulfilled? In spite of the market turmoil, I had a great opportunity in front of me. As history has shown, I would go through ups and downs and something seemed to be holding me back. I knew what I needed to do, but I just would not do it! I began to get extremely frustrated with myself. I knew I had the ability to be great, so I started reading books about the mind and how it works, as well as other self-help books and audio cd's. I wanted something better so badly, but it just wouldn't come. As a result, my income never grew and I faced eviction as well as more financial loss. I felt like a failure to my older kids, Kailee, and Jen.

As frustrated as I was, I did not give up and still pushed forward. One night, I had a mentor ask me, "What motivates you Tony? What really gets you excited?" That question was deep, so it took some time to really think about the answer. Then it hit me! I love helping people grow. I love to help people reach their goals, their dreams, their desires. At that moment, I began wondering if I was supposed to be some kind of coach or trainer. I got really excited about this new possibility, so I began looking into business and life coaching while I was working my financial practice.

In the middle of my struggles, I came to know God and was baptized in 2009. I never believed in any particular religion, nor did I give any thought on whether or not God existed, prior to baptism. At this point in my life, I was tired of being alone and having so much inner turmoil. It was then that I had an inner awakening. I wanted to get past a life of insignificance to gain a life of purpose and what I was currently doing was not working. Although it was rocky in the beginning, and still is from time to time, my spiritual enlightenment journey began with me accepting Jesus into my life and announcing this acceptance with that baptism.

In 2010 I got remarried to the mother of my youngest daughter, Kailee. Although the relationship and marriage was rocky at times, I was committed to becoming a better father and husband, despite my constant failings in that area. I was seeing some changes in my life, but still had some sharp edges that needed to be molded and shaped. I had no idea that my spiritual journey, and my inner transformation, were preparing me for the hardest thing I would ever have to encounter.

THE PAST FIVE YEARS

February 28, 2011 is a day that I will never forget. I can recall every little detail from that night. I can tell you in detail what I saw when I found her. I can tell you how horrible it felt when my heart sank to my stomach as I realized what was going on. I can tell you how hard it was to breathe as I grabbed my daughter to run upstairs to call 911. I can tell you how my heart crumbled and it felt like I was in a damn nightmare.

I do not discuss it in great detail as I do not want to relive the trauma, but that night will be forever etched deep into my mind. My wife was suffering from severe headaches that were worse than a migraine. Imagine your head being slowly squeezed in a vice while at the same time being hit repeatedly in one place with a hammer. That was the intensity of these headaches from what I was told from doctors and my wife. She took her medicine and laid down in an attempt to sleep. I let her rest the entire day and I took care of our daughter, Kailee, who was five at the time. I would check on her from time to time but I knew she needed to sleep.

As we did every night, Kailee and I would turn on her cartoons and watch them right before bed. The lights were out and the only light that emitted was from the TV. Kailee gave her mommy a kiss goodnight and covered her head up with the blanket. When I asked her why she covered her mommy she said "Mommy is cold so, I covered her up." I laughed and said "Well don't cover her head up, silly," and went to pull the blanket off my wife's head. When I did, I knew immediately that something didn't seem right and my heart began to sink.

I felt her head and she was cold. Granted, it was very cold in the house, but she was cold, too cold. I went to the top of the stairs and turned the lights on and when I checked on her again, my worst nightmare was realized. Jen was gone. I grabbed Kailee and ran upstairs gasping for air. I did not want Kailee to see her mommy like that. As we were running upstairs, Kailee fearfully asked me if mommy as going to be ok. The only thing I could respond with was "I don't know, sweetie," although I knew she wasn't going to be after what I witnessed. That image is forever engrained in my mind and do not want her or anyone else to ever have to live with that.

I immediately called 911 and it seemed like forever for the paramedics to arrive. It really only took maybe ten minutes for them to arrive, but it sure felt like it took an eternity. I say maybe ten minutes as I am not 100 percent clear as I was in complete shock, and I was on the phone with the 911 dispatch guiding me through CPR. I still remember hearing the words of the paramedic as he knelt down in front of me, "I am so sorry for your loss, she is in a better place now." At that moment, my heart shattered. She was only 30 years old and we had only been married for six months. Our daughter was without her mommy at just 5 years old. What do I do now? For I was completely, utterly, and hopelessly lost.

The next few months I was numb. Each day was a roller coaster, that I eagerly wanted to get off of. I would be overcome with extreme sadness and just cry, then came the anger. I would get so angry, particularly when I saw couples or families together. I was jealous of what they had. I wanted my wife back. I wanted my family back. I needed Jen. I even got mad at God for a while. The days I did have brief moments of happiness I felt guilty, like I was not supposed to be happy. It was an extremely hard time and I clang to Kailee as my rock. The first six months is where I felt God's presence the most. I was scared! Think back to the days when I was depressed and what I went through then. I did not want to go through that again, but what I was currently going through now was a million times worse than back then. Kailee needed me, but I was afraid.

After about six months of pain, loneliness, and living my worst nightmare over and over again each day, the days became a little more bearable and as part of my therapy, I would post encouraging quotes or phrases from a book I read on social media. People would begin responding with, "Thank you, I needed that." A couple of months after that, I had an epiphany. I remember one meeting I had with my pastor, with whom I met with often after Jen's death, and he told me that although he did not know completely what I was going through, he knows that God can make good out of bad, because God is good. Out of anger, I quickly responded with "how the hell can God make good out bad? He can't bring her back." His response was "I don't know, but I know He can."

That moment came to fruition when I realized my purpose in life. I finally knew why I was put here. My purpose was to help other people get past whatever was holding them back from having the life they desire. To help people find *their* purpose, their passion. To help them discover the life they were created for. Somehow God was going to use my loss to help others. I finished my certification as a life coach in late 2011, and began moving forward in order to help anyone and everyone. I didn't know the details, I just knew that I was supposed to move forward and things would fall into place. I met some great people along the way that guided me and encouraged me. I kept hearing "You need to find your niche", and I kept saying "But I can help everyone." I had many ups and downs moving forward and I just couldn't get my coaching practice off the ground. I needed money as I was struggling yet again, so I got back in to life insurance and eventually got a full-time job. I began to make excuses as to why I could not do coaching and got mad at God yet again. Maybe I wasn't supposed to be a coach? Maybe I was not good enough? I needed security in a job because I had a daughter to take care of and we needed a steady income.

Needless to say, the steady income was not enough so, I took some more risks to generate more income. As with the other risky maneuvers, this one backfired too. I had almost given up on the dream and lost some passion. There were some people who encouraged me to continue with coaching, but I continued to make excuses. I would try to do things here and there with coaching but I was not focused on it.

As I was attempting to move forward and establish a "new normal" in my life, my mom's health began to really deteriorate. For five years she was in an out of the hospital with illnesses caused by prolonged use to prescription pain medications. She was on the medicine due to an injury she sustained at work many years prior. The doctor that did the surgery messed up severely when attempting to repair the injury. This left my mom in severe pain, having to have more surgeries, and damage to her vital organs.

While my mom was in the hospital fighting for her life, my brother had a major heart attack and we almost lost him. For almost a month, I was traveling to two different hospitals to see my brother and my mom. My mom knew something was not right with my brother but we never told her what had happened. We still had hope that she would make it out of the hospital. After all, she faced death five times prior to that and made it through. A week prior to my mom passing, my brother came home.

Just two short years after my wife died, I watched my mom die in ICU. Her body could not handle any more. She was on a respirator and while she was of sound mind, we asked if she was ready to go see Jesus. She nodded "yes," so we honored her wishes, as hard as it was for my dad, brother, and I. Watching her die was extremely traumatic and it took over an hour despite the doctor stating it would not take more than ten minutes. Although my mom was worn out and ready to go, she was a fighter and fought until her last breath.

Shortly after my mom passed, I ended up getting remarried but that marriage ended in disaster. I will not say anything bad about her at all. At one point, I was very angry and bitter toward her for all that she said and did, but I have since forgiven her, letting all the anger and bitterness go, and wish her the absolute best. I will say that in a nutshell the marriage ended because when two hurt people get together, they hurt each other.

I am now very grateful that the marriage ended and I went through the suffering so that I could learn some valuable lessons. I know it's crazy to think that someone could be grateful for a failed marriage, but I am. I learned so much about myself and things I needed to change during that time that I am blessed having gone through it. I was finally able to get the healing I needed!

During the marriage, my anger came back out. I realized that the majority of my anger was because I tried to control every aspect of my life. I thought that if I could control everything, I was secure. This was a defense mechanism created deep on the subconscious level due to past failures and pain that I never fully dealt with. Consciously, I knew full well that it was impossible to control everything, yet my mind was trying to do so, which caused added stress to an already highly stressed environment.

I would try so hard not to get angry, but ultimately when you keep focusing on something you do not want, it is bound to happen. And it did. I was miserable. I hated the feeling of being angry, but could not figure out how to get past it. I was also getting angry because I felt like a failure in the eyes of my family. Again, the thoughts of not being good enough would creep back in.

After the marriage ended I was brought to my knees and my eyes were opened. I was finally aware of all my weaknesses that I either turned my back on or was ashamed of. The main one I wanted to deal with was my anger. I no longer wanted to be a slave to it. I watched my brother and dad become consumed by it that I no longer wanted it. I wanted peace for once in my life. It was hard to be transparent and vulnerable, especially for a guy. But I took the leap of faith and began speaking openly about it. The responses I received were the exact opposite of what I thought they would be. People did not judge me like I thought they would. Although I did not feel like someone that could inspire, they were inspired. They all had their own weaknesses and it gave them encouragement to deal with theirs. I immediately started to feel inner peace. A peace I could not explain.

Dealing with my anger and finding the inner peace and happiness I was looking for overflowed into other areas of my life. It strengthened my relationship with my daughter. It allowed me to focus on what mattered most, guiding her and helping her grow through love, not fear. I finally became content in my life. Not complacent, but content. I was okay with where I was and what I had in life. Of course I would get angry from time to time or frustrated, but I was able to recognize it quicker and either diffuse it quickly, or if I did stumble, quickly apologize and ask for forgiveness. I know I will never be perfect, but having a stronger self-awareness has brought me a long way. I would not have it if I did not go through the suffering I had endured.

My goal is to continue to grow as a person and a father. I have failed as a father many times, especially with my older ones. I have learned from those mistakes and want to change how I do things. I want my daughter to respect me out of love, not fear. I know when she gets older, she will ultimately choose a guy that is like me. A question I often ask myself is "If Kailee were to choose a guy like me right now, would I be happy with that choice?" For the longest time, the answer to that question was "Hell no!" Asking that question is my drive to become a better person and an even better dad. I want her to grow up and have the knowledge and mental toughness to deal with any hardship that comes her way. I want to speak life into her and build her up, not tear her down.

I am no longer stressed like I used to be. My anxiety has been minimized and often times it is nonexistent. I know that I will stumble but I am adamant about seeking growth. I do not give up. I get back up and I go at it again. I will continue to do so as long as I am breathing.

Raising a daughter with Post Traumatic Stress Disorder (PTSD) is not easy. It is not easy for either of us. I have PTSD as well. Everything reminds her of her mommy. She will often be overcome by grief and cry asking for her mommy to come back. She will even say "I want a new mommy. When is God going to bring me a new mommy?" As a dad, this crushes me. I want to take her pain away and I can't. All I can do is hold her and comfort her, and say "When God says its time, he will bring the right person into our life. For now, we need this time together to grow and become stronger." Many times after she calms down, I will get her some ice cream or candy. Ice cream makes everyone happy. Most of the time I just hold her and pray as I fight back the tears. This has become our new normal as I like to call it.

As a single parent it is already hard to play both roles. Add trauma to the mix and it becomes that much harder. I often tell her that we are a team and we will get through this together. I take her to get pedicures and yes, I get one with her. Real men get pedicures with their daughters. I play dolls with her. I watch her Disney movies with her and act out the parts with her. Personally, I think dads should connect with their daughters on this level even if mom is in the picture. I am constantly creating new memories with her because memories are important to the growth and well-being of a child, especially one who has experienced so much trauma in such a short period of time.

School can be a whole other issue. She struggles in school because it is hard for her to focus. Everything triggers a memory of her mom. She has a hard time being away from home and sleeping in her own bed because the fear is so great. I even wake up multiple times in the middle of the night and check to make sure she is breathing. This is what trauma does to a person. It affects everyone differently. Knowing the truth consciously is completely different than what trauma causes subconsciously. Trauma does not know the difference between reality and make believe. The struggle is real. But we deal with it. We adapt. We adjust. We make the best of it. We are becoming stronger everyday as a result.

From all that I have experienced and learned, I have decided to take a stand. I am taking a stand that my life and my daughter's life will be different, our lives will be extraordinary. I have decided that I am changing my family tree. I watched my dad fall apart after my mom passed. He ended up having triple bypass surgery and later had congestive heart failure several times. He was stricken with grief, but also lives with the burden of anger. I watched my brother go through two major heart attacks. I am declaring that this will not happen to me. I have chosen to change how I feel, how I act, and how I respond to others and situations. I will love deeper, I will live fuller, and I will make a difference in the lives of others, starting with mine and my daughter's! And by God's grace and strength, I will succeed.

CHAPTER ONE

YOU ARE NOT
DEFINED BY YOUR PAST

iving in the past is what causes depression. Thinking about the past
is the same as living in the past. We all have a past, some worse than
others, but we all have one. What does living in the past accomplish
besides doubt, regret, shame, and depression? Why do we allow ourselves to become our pasts? Better yet, when did we become our pasts?
Is our past who we really are? These are great questions that have
equally great answers. If you are someone that is stuck in their past
and imprisoned by their past I want you to know this: there is hope.

You are not your past. It has made you who you are today, but it
is not you. You are not the mistakes you made. You are not the sum
of your past mistakes. You are more than your past. You are stronger
than your past. You are the person you are today because of your
past, but you are not your past. The only one that can control you is
you. No one, or anything, can control you unless you allow it to.

The past also does not mean it is your present or your future. Just
because something happened in the past, does not mean it will happen again. The mistakes you made in the past are learning experiences to grow from so you don't continue making the same mistakes.
What if you continue to make the same mistake? Does that make you
a failure? No! Does that mean that is who you are? No! You keep trying until you get passed it.

You are not defined by your past so don't wallow in it. When we
remain "stuck" in the past, we can very easily (and often do) take

on the "victim" mentality. We get the mindset of "bad things just happen to me", or "this is how my life has always been", or "nothing ever seems to go right." The list can go on and on. It does not matter how bad your past is, or what you have been through. You can break free and move away from it. We are designed to learn from our past, make changes, and to grow. This process continues until the day we die. We are human. We will always make mistakes. Bad things are going to happen to us. We learn from those mistakes and misfortunes and move forward one step at a time.

I think it's wise to point out again that we are in control of ourselves. We cannot control our outside world, but we can control us. We cannot control what happens to us, but we can control how we react to it. We cannot change what has already passed, but we can change what we do today based on what happened in the past. Life is a learning game. We take chances. We make plays that we think are great and end up in disaster. Some plays are amazing. Maybe we had a momentary lapse in judgment. Maybe we were around the wrong people and wanted to fit-in and made bad choices. It does not matter what has happened in the past. It is the past. There is a reason we have a small rearview mirror and a huge windshield in our vehicles. We are supposed to do more looking forward than looking back. We need to reflect, make the necessary adjustments and move forward.

Our pasts are a chance for us to grow. I believe I have mentioned this before. This is important to understand. Instead of being ashamed of our pasts, we need to embrace them. There is so much wisdom to be gained from our past. I know some amazing people that do amazing things that have unbelievable pasts. Pasts that take you by surprise when they share them. Pasts you wonder how they are where they are right now. There really is no wondering. It's simple. It's because they *chose* not to let it consume them. They did not allow their past to rule them and keep them shackled or imprisoned. They broke free and are now empowered to live a life of purpose and significance.

When we remain in our past and allow it to control our present, we are robbing ourselves of the blessings of today. We are allowing our past to shape our future. It does not matter what happened in the past. All that matters is what you want today. Who you want to be today. Who you want to be remembered as. Use your past as a tool to help others in similar situations. It's crazy to think that our pasts can be a powerful tool to shape the future in a positive way, but first we have to change our perspective on how we view our past. We have to change the meaning of our past.

How do we change the meaning? We no longer take it personal. When we detach ourselves from whatever it is that's holding us back, we are free to observe in a nonjudgmental way. We can see the past for what it is, a past. Not our present. Not our future. When we can change the meaning, we let go of the bitterness, shame, anger, guilt, or whatever emotion we have attached to it. It no longer has an effect on us.

The second thing to remember is to not let others hold your past against you either. If they do, you need to run away as fast as you can. If it's hard to get away from them, maybe they are family, then you just ignore them or limit the time you spend with them. Again, everyone has their own past, so how can they hold something against us that's in the past? It's easy to do if we are living in the past. The moment we stop, the moment we change the meaning, is the moment our past no longer binds us. If we can change the meaning. If we can break free from our past, then people can no longer use it against us. They may still try to bring it up, or talk behind our backs, but that is their issue, not ours. God does not hold your past against you, so why should you allow yourself, or anyone else to hold it against you?

The third thing to remember is that you are stronger because of your past. You can take bad things and make great things out of them. The bad that goes on in our lives can be used exponentially for the greater good of ourselves and for mankind. Think about that for a moment. Our bad can be used to make a difference in the lives of others. That is deep! That is powerful! That is the absolute truth. We are here for a purpose. Each and everyone one of us has one. When we focus on the past, we stray from the path of our purpose. Your past is not you, you are good enough, and you deserve to accomplish great things. When we remain in the past, we are preventing ourselves from achieving our true purpose. Make the decision to break the shackles today and break out of the prison that is your past, and jump onto the path of the real you.

What would it feel like if you let go of your past right now? Would it be peaceful? Physically, how would you feel? Would your body be more relaxed? Envision your past as a bag of luggage you are carrying around. It may seem light at first, right? But as time goes on and we are constantly carrying the bag it gets heavier, doesn't it? And at the same time, we are adding more to it which is adding to that weight. Imagine putting all of the stress, pain, bitterness, anger, all the negative emotions you are feeling, into that luggage. Can you feel the weight of it now? Now imagine you just drop the luggage. How does letting go of all the years of living in the past feel? That's what it feels like to let go.

That is all we have to do. We have to drop the luggage. The process will take time and we will have to recondition our habits and behaviors in our brain, but the decision is instantaneous. You may even feel a sense of peace relief when you make the decision. The moment we make the decision to not allow our past to define who we are and believe the lie we have been telling ourselves, is the moment that changes begin to take place in our brain. If this is where you are today, I would like to challenge you to drop your luggage and take the first step forward to your new beginning.

I let the past consume me for years. It dictated almost everything I did. My relationships, my work, my well-being, everything. All my past failures overruled what I was really capable of. I had dreams. I had desires. But my past would creep in under the radar and sabotage my efforts. In college, when I suffered from depression and anxiety, I was living in the past. I was living with my dad not showing up at my high school graduation. Subconsciously my mind went to graduating college and my dad not being there either. Since I felt like nothing in his eyes, I always tried to prove myself to him. Maybe not on a conscious level, but that is what I was doing.

Every time I failed at an entrepreneurial venture, it stayed with me. Every time I failed financially (usually as the result of an entrepreneurial venture) the failure would stay with me. Every failed relationship would be carried forward. Much of my past lived in my subconscious and I was not aware that I was sabotaging myself. When I stated earlier that I knew I wanted more, but something seemed to hold me back, this is what that something was. I was being held back from all my past mistakes. I was being held back from every bad choice. Whether it was in my control or not, it was there holding me back. I was being held back by my negative programming, some caused by me, and some programmed from a young age.

I would fear stepping forward and taking new risks because of my past even though I knew the risk would be so much better for me. I settled for "security" because I just knew the result would be the same if I tried anything new. I became a prisoner of my past which caused a new anxiety, anger, and sadness to corrupt my true self. I began to feel that I was just not meant to have a great life. That I would just be someone who struggled through life and not get very far. I began to give up on my dreams. I would tell myself that I just was not good enough. Subconsciously the "You're stupid" thoughts and the "you will not ever amount to anything," was holding me back.

My failures as a dad, a son, a business person, and a husband all weighed on me. The regrets consumed me. No matter how much I was doing to grow and become better, it was never good enough because I was still living in my past. Instead of celebrating my growth in those areas, I would zero it out with negative self-talk. As a result, my confidence and self-esteem diminished. I seemed happy on the outside, but on the inside, I was miserable. Even so, something deep inside longed for something more. But what was it and how could I get there?

It was not until I changed the meaning of certain life events, until I stopped seeking approval from others, until I let go of the past as a failure and viewed my past as a learning tool that things began to change. It took a major crisis to bring me to my knees, to really open my eyes to what was really going on. It is amazing how God uses our worst times to bring the greatest growth in our lives. All it takes is a change in perception and an awareness to free us to begin to realize our full potential.

I also lived with certain people attempting to bring my past up, constantly throwing it in my face. These people were relentless. A couple of them still try to bring it up to this day, but I no longer take part in it. Who are they to throw my past in my face? It happened and nothing can be done. They have their own past so who are they to judge me? I no longer allow them, or anyone, to use my past against me. I don't give them control. I eliminated them from my life or I choose to ignore them. I am so much more than that, and so are you! I am not saying that it is easy to ignore, but just like anything else, it takes conditioning. I had to develop an awareness to notice when I was being defined by my past or allowing someone else to define me by my past. I refuse to allow anyone to use my past against me, including myself.

I finally realized that the past is the past and I define my life by where my focus is. I am now thankful for all the mistakes I made and the challenges I went through because it made me who I am today. I would not be the man I am today if I did not go through all of that. I am a stronger version of the real me. I am not that person of the past. I use my past as a tool for growth, not as a tool to hinder me.

ACTION STEPS

1. Drop the luggage of the past you have been carrying around so long. No longer allow it to hold you back from who you really are.

2. Change the meaning of your past experiences. View them as learning experiences to help you grow, instead of chains that hold you down.

3. Stop allowing others to hold your past against you. Rediscover who you really are deep down inside, the you that was put on the earth to do extraordinary things.

CHAPTER TWO
FORGIVENESS

Forgiveness is often misunderstood and overused at the same time. The word is thrown out quite often but what does "forgiveness" really mean? *What* does forgiveness really do? *Who* is forgiveness really for? *How* do you forgive? These are just a few of the many questions that have gone through my head and I am quite certain has gone through yours as well.

I believe that if everyone really understood what forgiveness is and how to apply it to their life, relationships would be healed and this world would be a much better place. Forgiveness can be powerful if used as it was intended. I think of it as the key that opens the door to a more peaceful and fulfilled life. The door that leads to the path of the life we were all created for, whatever that may be.

It is often believed that you have to feel ready to forgive someone, but if you're not ready to forgive then you don't forgive. Forgiveness takes time. Part of that belief is true while the other part is incorrect. Forgiveness does not come when you feel it; it is a choice. It is a choice to let go of the burden that holds us down from the hurts others have caused, or from what we have done, or even what the world has done. We *choose* to forgive. If we sit around and wait to "feel" like forgiving, we may never get there. Why? Because the bitterness, anger, and pain from whatever happened is still there and most likely becoming stronger. Eventually the bitterness, anger, and pain will consume us. We may even act like we're over it with time, but in reality, if it is not dealt with, it never goes away. Time does not heal the open wounds, which are the past hurts and the pain of regrets. The pain just gets stored down into our subconscious and comes out through self-sabotage, through anger, through bitterness, through declining health, and many other negative emotions and experiences.

We often mistake forgiveness as saying that what the other person did was okay. Forgiveness does not mean we are letting the other person off the hook. What is really going on when we forgive, is that we are letting ourselves off the hook. Do you think the person that hurt you is still thinking about the time they hurt you? Most likely not. Is it possible the other person does not even know they hurt you? Yes. Forgiving someone does not mean it was okay for what they did. It means we are letting go of the baggage that not forgiving allows us to carry.

We also do not have to continue to be in a relationship with the person that hurt us. There may be instances where continuing the relationship just is not feasible, or healthy. Ideally, it is best to physically tell the person that you forgive them. If it is not possible, maybe the person has died or is too toxic to be around, forgiveness can still take place.

The most important element to remember about forgiveness is that forgiveness is for us, not anyone else. It is for us and us alone. Forgiveness sets us free. It breaks the chains that enslave us. It allows healing to take place by removing all the anger, the resentment and the bitterness that has been pent up inside of us. All the junk that is slowly destroying us. It will bring more joy and peace into our lives. Not just outwardly, but an inner peace that comes from deep within our souls.

If you have not forgiven yourself for your past, or present for that matter, do it now. Physically tell yourself out loud that you forgive yourself and state specifically why you forgive yourself. Then state that you are no longer going to allow the past to control you. Finally, state that you choose to let this go. Ask God to help you let it go. Forgive yourself for holding on to your past. Forgive yourself for holding on to the pain that someone else caused. Forgive yourself for being angry at God for taking a loved one away too soon. Before you can forgive anyone else, you have to forgive yourself first. Everything starts with you first before it can go out to others.

By being specific you are breaking the link between the unre-solved forgiveness and your subconscious. By forgiving yourself, you are beginning the process of forgiveness. You will not be able to "feel" like forgiving until you actually forgive. Many think that it is the exact opposite. You have to forgive in order to feel.

Notice I said "process." Forgiveness is instantaneous, but the pro-cess takes time. New neuropaths have to be formed in the brain so it will take some time for the process to complete. Each time the past hurt begins to creep into your mind, firmly say to yourself "no, I have already forgiven that hurt and I let it go." Continue this until the process is complete. Over time you will see that these times will get further and further apart and the peace will get deeper. You will feel the weight roll off of you. It is very possible that when you begin the process, you will immediately begin to feel relief. You may even cry. That is perfectly normal and part of the healing process.

Once you have forgiven yourself, you can take the same process and apply it to other people, especially those that you cannot physically forgive. Again, if you have the opportunity to forgive the person, do so directly with them. Relationships can be rekindled simply by forgiving. Marriages can be restored through forgiveness. Just like working out, as you practice forgiveness, it will become easier and easier.

Just as we forgive others, it may be necessary to ask for forgive-ness from others. To ask for forgivenss from God. Just as we have been hurt by others, we have hurt others as well. Maybe it's our chil-dren. Maybe it's our spouse. Maybe it's a family member. You get the point. Holding on to regret will consume us. Reach out and ask for forgiveness if you can. If you are unable to ask for whatever reason, simply pray for forgiveness and that the other person forgives you.

Now, for something really surprising. What if I told you that forgiv-ing in one area of your life will actually lead to growth in other areas of your life as well? All areas of our life are connected together and one influences the other. If you have unresolved personal conflict, it can roll over into your relationships, into our jobs or businesses, even into our health. By simply forgiving yourself of your past can have a huge impact on other areas of your life. I once heard a story of a man who owned his own business, but the business stopped growing. Through exploration, it came known that the man was still very angry with his ex-wife for the divorce. He did not see the connection between the built up anger with his wife and his lack of growth within his business. After some nudging, the man decided to forgive his former wife. The following year, his business doubled! This is one of many examples of how forgiveness has a profound impact on all areas of our lives.

One of the hardest practices of forgiveness is to forgive those that continue to hurt us in the present. But you must remember: forgiveness is for us. So when this person says hurtful things to us, brings up our past, or spreads lies about us, we need to forgive them. I know this is very hard to do, but it can be done. Our first instinct is to defend ourselves. But all that does is give them control of our emotions. We do not need to defend ourselves. We ignore the attacks and forgive them. In the moment, it is extremely hard to do. It will take hard work, and strong awareness to master, so be easy on yourself if you stumble. I still stumble in this area too. We are human and will get angry from time to time. We will get frustrated from time to time. That is normal. What is not normal is staying in that state for a long period of time.

Forgiveness is the key to letting go of our past. It is the key to having a fulfilled life, a life we desire. It is a process that if followed, will bring great joy and peace to our lives. If we do not practice forgiveness, we will be consumed by the negative emotions and baggage that comes along by holding on to past hurts and regret. By not forgiving, we are missing out on all the blessings this life has to offer. Forgiveness is essential to having the life you were created for. Do not rob yourself of an extraordinary life by not forgiving. Your relationships will be stronger, and you will be stronger by forgiving.

Forgiveness has been a godsend for me. I used to be one of those guys that would stay mad at someone for a very long time and hold grudges. All the hurt of my past and from others consumed me. The whole reason I became depressed and had anxiety is because I held on to old hurts. I became bitter although I tried to hide it or ignore it. I used to tell myself "I'm fine" and "It's done and over with" when in reality, I was still hurting inside.

I used to believe that you had to feel like forgiving someone before you could actually forgive that person. And in most cases that feeling never came along. In many other instances, I would "let it go" but deep down the scar was still there. Eventually it would rear its ugly head again. It became a vicious cycle. If someone said something hurtful to me, I would think about it over and over and the anger and resentment and bitterness would get stronger and stronger. I would play it over and over in my head. I would think of scenarios of how I would hurt them back and the things I would say to them. It would literally cause excess anxiety and stress. It was a horrible feeling to hold on to.

I hated the way I felt and the way I thought. I would often say "I forgive you," or "I am better than that and am not letting what they say hurt me." Whoever said "sticks and stones may break my bones, but words will never hurt me" is a liar! Words hurt deeply and if we allow them to, they can control our lives. I used to "ignore" and blow it off. After a few days, the thoughts would subside until I would get stressed out again. The stress did not even have to be related to the original issue, but all the past hurts, words, and events would creep right back into my mind sending my anxiety through the roof. I often wondered why past hurts would come up on a completely unrelated subject. I later realized that once we go into a negative state, all unresolved negative feelings and events would come to the surface again. Until we completely resolve the pain, they will continue to resurface over and over and over again.

One day, in the middle of my last divorce when I decided to take control of everything, I did some research on forgiveness. After this research I had a new awareness about my past and about the people who hurt me, past and present. I realized that much of my anger was from my past. Because I never really forgave them or myself for that matter, I was angry. I no longer wanted anything to do with the anger or hurt. I went through the process of forgiveness beginning with myself. I knew that I had to forgive myself before I could really forgive anyone else.

I did not feel like forgiving but I sure did not want to feel the way I was feeling anymore. I was ready to try anything at this point because what I was doing was not serving me anymore. I forgave myself for my past. My past failures. My past mistakes as a father.

My past mistakes as a son. My past mistakes as a husband. I forgave myself for allowing others to use my past against me, allowing others to control my feelings. I forgave myself for all the regret of not seeking my dreams. For giving up on my dreams. For not believing I was good enough. For all the hurt I caused others at some point.

When I began forgiving myself, I cried. I grieved my past at that moment. When I was done, I had a peace come over me that is unexplainable. I felt like a weight had just lifted off my shoulders and I could breathe again. And I thought to myself, "this is all I had to do?" It was simple yet hard at the same time. I believe we have to go through hard times to really gain clarity. We grow the most in our darkest moments. By forgiving myself, I was able to begin the healing and forgiveness process. This process takes time. I did not get that way over night and I sure was not going to recondition myself overnight. I still have doubts. I still look at my past from time to time. It typically will come back when I am about to do something that is moving me forward in my life. When I am seeking something larger than me. I quickly remind myself that I forgave myself and the past is not who I am. I tell myself no, and remind myself of who I am and what I am capable of.

One area I still struggle with is forgiving those who continue to try and hurt me or say things that are not true. I realize that we are all going to have people who will try to bring us down in this life and we have to learn to ignore them although it is extremely hard. My natural instinct is to defend myself when someone is saying things that are not true. I have learned that I give that person control when I do that. I do not need to defend myself. I know the truth and those that really know me, know the truth. Hurt people hurt people. Period! When someone is miserable inside, the easiest way for them to feel better about themselves is to tear someone else down. When we are doing something great for ourselves and for others, you best believe you are going to have people say something negative. Forgiving them and ignoring them is not easy though. It takes practice. I used to be so hard on myself when I stumbled in this area. I would forgive myself then forgive them and continue to remind myself of the forgiveness until the feeling would subside. It has gotten easier for me but that is because it's a constant practice. I am strengthening my mental muscle and increasing my awareness. Be easy on yourself as you practice forgiveness on a daily basis.

ACTION STEPS

1. Forgive yourself. Forgive yourself of your past. All your past hurts and regrets. Forgive yourself for anything that is holding you back. Be specific. Speak it out loud. Tell yourself that you forgive you and be specific as to what you are forgiving for. State that you are no longer allowing it to control you. Finally, say that you choose to let it go. Until the process is complete, every time the hurt comes up say, "No, I already forgave for that, I choose to let it go."

2. Make a list of 3 people that you need to forgive (i. e. ex-spouses, children, old friend, etc.). Then follow the process in step one to forgive each person. If you can forgive them in person, that is the best way, but not necessary.

CHAPTER THREE

HAPPINESS COMES FROM WITHIN

We all seek happiness in some way. We were created to seek happiness and pleasure. We automatically gravitate toward things that bring us pleasure and do everything in our power to avoid pain. Society has taught us that happiness comes from the outside world. We believe that other people make us happy. We believe that more money will bring us more happiness. We believe that guy or lady will bring us more happiness. If I could only get that new car, that new TV, that new gadget, I would be happy.

We have been conditioned to seek happiness from the outside. From drugs and alcohol to shopping. From having sex with someone to seeking attention from other people. In reality none of those things bring true happiness. The happiness that comes from the outside is temporary. It does not last. And once it fades we are off seeking the next thing to bring us happiness. And we continue this vicious cycle and fall short of finding true, lasting, happiness.

We put all our hope in that lady or guy and begin the "honeymoon" phase. The problem is that people let people down. And the first time this person lets us down, the happiness goes away and we become unhappy. We begin seeking happiness elsewhere. In some instances, we may not leave the other person, but sabotage the relationship to justify leaving or force them to leave.

Don't get me wrong, we were created to be in relationships. Strong and healthy relationships personally and professionally. Quality relationships are key to our growth and overall fulfillment. But they are not the center of our happiness. Happiness through relationships alone is not sustainable. Happiness through obtaining more money is not sustainable. There is nothing wrong with money, but if we focus on getting more money and tie that to our happiness, we will never reach it. We will always be telling ourselves, if I can make x amount of money I will be happy. Once we hit x amount, we will raise the bar. We will continue to raise that bar and never be satisfied and most likely have problems in other areas of our lives. We try to find happiness through buying more things. Keeping up with the Joneses. We continue accumulating things but remain unhappy.

We have to find happiness in a more lasting way. But how? Where does happiness come from? The answer: Happiness comes from within each and every one of us. We have the power to create happiness in our lives through getting in touch with our inner selves. When we search deep within, we are led to the source of all happiness: God. We are spiritually connected to Him and send off energy and attract back like energy. Our hearts are the biggest source of that energy and what you feel in your heart is what you will receive back.

It takes a strong awareness to really look inside to find that happiness. It takes healing to bring awareness to open your heart to receive the happiness you seek. What type of healing? Healing from your past. Forgiving others and yourself. Forgiveness, letting go of your past, and true happiness are all tied together.

Happiness comes by letting go of what we cannot control. By leaning on God and trusting the plan he has for us. By responding to outside forces versus reacting to outside forces. When we respond to the outside forces, we are in control, when we react to the outside forces, we are not in control. We have to learn to control how we respond to situations. We all face hard times, some more and worse than others, but we all face them. The difference between those that make it through and those that do not, is how they respond. If we allow life to knock us around, we will never find happiness.

We have to learn to be happy with ourselves before we can be happy with other people or things. If we are hurt and broken, we will continue to hurt other people then blame the other person. We will attract hurt and broken people. We do not see that we are the cause. It may be possible that the other person has their own faults but we are only in control of ourselves. Remember, the energy we put off through our hearts attracts the same energy back. If we are not happy with what we are attracting into our lives, instead of continuing to look elsewhere, we need to look within and look up. The answers are always within us.

Happiness comes by living our passion and purpose. If we are in line with our purpose and living intentionally in our purpose, happiness will fill us. If we are living in our values and really know who we are, we will find happiness. Often times, we lose sight of who we are for many different reasons. If this is where you are now, there is hope. It often takes going through something very difficult to open our eyes. Maybe that is where you are right now. But it doesn't have to take something tragic to open your eyes. Take the time to search yourself. Get to know yourself. If you have lost yourself, seek yourself. Seek what moves you. Search for what gets you excited. Find your why!

Be true to yourself. Do not be anyone other than yourself. Be authentic. Set boundaries with yourself and others. Do not deviate from who you are at your core. By deviating you will find a great deal of unhappiness. You will feel the inner struggle and it will cause stress and anxiety. It will consume you. Do not let this happen. If you are in this state right now, break the pattern. Seek a coach to help you navigate and get you back in touch with the awesome person that has been lost if you are struggling in this area.

By creating happiness within, we will begin to attract opportunities and the right people into our lives. It almost seems impossible, but it is by design. It is from the energy we are putting out as a result of the changes God is doing inside of us. This process takes time and practice. It takes patience. It will not be easy in the beginning. It takes some "soul searching" to find out who you really are. If you have lost who you are, you may be searching for a while. While searching, ask yourself empowering questions like "Who am I?" and "What am I passionate about?" The answers will eventually come to you. Do not get discouraged and do not give up. You deserve it and it's yours. You just have to grab a hold of it. I promise that the time it takes to find your happiness is well worth it. It is worth the joy. It is worth the peace. It is worth the growth you will see in all areas of your life.

I struggled with happiness for years. To be honest, I struggled up until about a year and a half prior to writing this book. Although you couldn't tell from the outside most of the time, I was in a dark place. I never really understood what true happiness was or where it came from. Like most of the world, I was seeking happiness in other people and other things.

I was also financially unhappy so I was constantly seeking the new job or the new business venture. I would become quickly dissatisfied and flake out. Some of my "flaking" came in the form of self-sabotage from "not being good enough." That feeling came from holding on to past failures, people telling me I couldn't do it, or was not ready, and holding on to being "stupid and never amounting to anything." On the surface, I seemed fine, but I was miserable on the inside and my subconscious was really in control.

I also sought happiness with new things so I would go shopping to feel better. I wanted the latest and greatest things, the nice car, newer clothes, etc. I wanted to keep up with the Joneses. Like so many others, I really was not in a financial position to keep up with anyone but myself. Instead of saving, I would just buy on emotion and justify why it was okay and why I needed it.

I then began to seek happiness in other people. I would date others thinking this one would be the right person. Because I was not happy with myself, I couldn't possibly be happy with anyone else. I would either break it off, or the person was not a good fit and we did not get along for any number of reasons. Also, because I was unhappy, I would be attracted to other unhappy women. I finally realized that I could not be intimately involved with someone that was not emotionally strong. I was attracted to the person I knew they could be, the potential they had, but not who they were presently. You cannot be involved with someone for their potential. Until they are that person, it's better for you not date them. The ones that were healthy, I was either horrible to (pushing them away to justify why it did not work out), or I would just break it off.

I needed to heal and strengthen myself emotionally before I could find the right person for me. I had to let go of the past. I had to forgive myself and other people. I had to let go of old patterns and behaviors that no longer served me and replace those with new patterns and behaviors that served me in a more fulfilling way. I had to learn to really love me and be happy with me. I had to lean on God more and less on me. I had to gain an awareness in order to see what was wrong. It took my wife walking out on us for the last time for me to finally realize it. I became intentional about being by myself and began to focus on healing and becoming a better dad.

In order for me to really show up the best I could for others, I had to be selfish for a short period of time. Sometimes we have to put the brakes on in our lives and take time for ourselves. Many of us are so focused on making other people happy that we forget about our own happiness. That is what I mean by being selfish. But it's selfish in a way that will allow us to serve people in a greater capacity.

I want to be the best version I can be in order to attract the right person for me. A healthy person that is on the same level. Relationships take a lot of work, so when one or both are not emotionally strong, then the relationship is that much harder or more likely to not last. I am in a great place now. For the first time in my life I am happy with myself, where I am headed, and happy being alone. It takes these things to happen before being able to be happy with anyone else. I still have work to do, but that will always be the case while I'm still on this earth. I will not stop working on personal growth and seeking a deeper and deeper happiness.

Because I have found inner happiness and have healed, I am now in a better position to attract opportunities and fulfill my passion and purpose. I no longer need to chase the next "shiny" thing that will bring me happiness. Of course I want money and nice things, but I don't need them to make me happy. I am the "shiny" thing and can now go down the path I was created for. Of course I will still get down. Everyone does. We are human. The difference is that I won't stay down and it will not affect my relationships in a negative way. The reason I am able to write this book is because of where my heart is. Find your happiness and watch your life grow exponentially!

ACTION STEPS

1. Take some time to reflect on where you are seeking your happiness. If it is anywhere other than from within, stop and search within. What is the root cause of your unhappiness? Change the story you are telling yourself. Choose to create happiness in all circumstances.

2. Take some time to be selfish. Spend some time to make sure you are happy. If you are spending more time making others happy and neglecting your own happiness, you are setting yourself up for failure.

3. Discover who you really are and your values. What do you stand for? What lights you up when you think, or talk about it? (If you need help in this area, I recommend hiring a coach that can get you results quicker than you can on your own.... by the way, I know a great coach! ☺)

CHAPTER FOUR

BEING CONTENT WHERE YOU ARE

Before you can be content where you are, I believe you have to be content with who you are. They work hand in hand because as you are working on who you are, you become content with where you are.

I want to be clear, content where you are does not mean being complacent with where you are. It does not mean that we stop seeking growth. We always have to seek growth if we want to continue to move forward, change and become a better version of ourselves. It means that we are okay where we are as we seek to achieve what we desire.

Let me explain, if you are not happy with your current financial situation, be content where you are first while you seek to change your situation. You will never reach your goal if you are not content. As a matter of fact, you will never become content and will continue to be dissatisfied no matter what your financial situation becomes. You will continue to chase the next "new opportunity" and never reach your full potential. You will make unnecessary mistakes along the way that can harm your financial situation further. It will most likely affect other areas of your life as well. This holds true for any area of life we are not content with.

Our greatest growth arises from a place of contentment. We become more aware of our weaknesses and other areas of improvement that were hidden because our focus was all over the place. We begin to see things about ourselves that we weren't able to see before.

It is an awareness that is beyond us, yet in us at the same time. Being content reduces stressful situations and increases our ability to be patient. I know for many, "patience" can be a foreign word.

We have become so focused on everything else, and chasing this, and chasing that, that we cause anxiety to fester which increases our irritability, our disappointment, and our unhappiness. It is a vicious cycle that will not end until we can learn to be content. We have to break the cycle. Sometimes it takes going through dark times to open our eyes, to bring us to our knees. Many times, we have to go through hard times multiple times until it finally hits us right between the eyes.

Prior to contentment, we may experience some growth, but it doesn't occur fast enough which is discouraging and can even cause a momentary relapse. Once healing and forgiveness enters, and we find true happiness, contentment follows which opens the floodgates to endless opportunities for growth.

We begin to attract amazing opportunities into our lives and we begin gaining exponential forward momentum. We find that our passions return and dreams are re-kindled. We start feeling that energy we once lost and others around us start noticing a difference. They see that sparkle in our eyes and the pep in our step, and the excitement in our voices as we talk about where we are in our lives and where we want to go. We gain more clarity on life, who we are, and what we want. What we truly want. We are better to define who we are and what we value.

Being content allows us to be grateful for what we have. Grateful for what we have gone through and the lessons learned as a result. We become grateful for going through the tough times because it made us who we are. It allows us to be more humble as we seek out our re-kindled passions and dreams. When we are grateful and humble, abundance appears. Not just abundance financially, I mean abundance in all areas of our lives. That's what true abundance is, balance in all areas of our lives. We are content in our relationships, our career or business, spiritually, with our giving, etc. The common denominator in all of this is US. The change starts with us. Nothing in our outside world will ever change unless we change our inside world. If you are unhappy with how things are in any area of your life, examine yourself first. Are you content in your life right now? If your answer is no, no amount of money, no new business adventure or career, no new relationship, no new nothing, is going to change it.

Be content where you are first, and watch how every area of your life will begin to be blessed. You will be able to choose the right person as a partner. You will choose a better career, business opportunities, you will make more rational decisions. Your health will improve. It becomes a ripple effect that touches every area of your life. It will even begin to touch others as well.

I want you to realize that this is also a process. You can't just wake up one day and say "all right, I'm content." It takes practice, patience, and intentionality. It takes a shift in mindset. It takes breaking patterns physically, emotionally and physiologically. How we walk, how we talk, and how we carry ourselves all takes part in this process. We have to recondition our thinking and be intentional. This takes an awakening, an awareness that is deeper than you have ever experienced. It takes reaching a higher level of consciousness, a deepening with your higher self, divine being, God, whatever you choose to call it. I choose to call it getting closer and more in tune with God through Jesus.

You have to speak about what you want in life and turn away from anything that is against it. Seek healing. Seek growth. Get laser focused on your goals and tell others what you want. Reflect often. I would say reflect daily, but it does not necessarily have to be daily. Over time you will change and one day you will realize that you are content. You will smile. You may cry and that is okay, they will be happy tears. Tears of joy! It's a great feeling and well worth the work.

Up until a short time ago, I was not content. I would say I was and I would act like I was for a short period of time, but I would eventually gravitate back to my old ways. I was so un-content that it would stress me out causing my lack of contentment to increase. I believed I was okay and would justify why I was making a change, or I would blame others for why I was not happy. I would do this over and over until I actually believed it. Don't get me wrong, in some cases the people, or jobs were not a good fit. But it all boiled down to me. My outside world was a reflection of my inside world. I was unable to attract quality people or jobs because I was not content, for the most part. I did have some quality people in my life, and I did have some good job opportunities, but overall I was unable to attract the right people or opportunities due to my lack of satisfaction.

I would start something new and I would be overly excited. I would see some success, but it was not what I thought it would be, or I was not moving as fast I thought I would. I would become unhappy. The more I thought about the unhappiness, the unhappier I would be come. I would lose interest and begin seeking the next best opportunity. In reality, any of those could have been great but I was not satisfied. I got a degree in accounting and worked in an office. I was happy for a while but then got bored. In this case I knew I was meant for more than just sitting behind a desk. But instead of really taking the time to analyze what I wanted, I went for the next best thing. Some of these opportunities were great, but once again, I would not see the success I felt I should be achieving and I would lose motivation.

In some instances, I wanted to do more but something was holding me back. I never could quite figure it out. I would reason that it just was not the right opportunity for me. Since I became unsatisfied yet again, I searched for the next best thing to fulfill me. I would self-improve by reading books, going to seminars, listening to audio CDs, etc., yet I was still stuck. I would see some growth but not enough.

Because I would become so unsatisfied, I would get involved in other business opportunities to make more money only to find myself unhappy and in more debt. I would begin to work myself out of it and do it all over again. I began to get discouraged and began to believe that I was not meant to be successful and was here to struggle and that was my purpose. Not great reasoning, or purpose, but that is the point I got to. I began to settle. The more I settled, the more dissatisfied I got.

My intimate relationships were the same way. I would either choose those that were emotionally unhealthy, subconsciously of course, or I would sabotage those that didn't. Just as with jobs and business opportunities, I would go to the next relationship thinking this was the one. Even the relationships that I did not explicitly cause to fail, I did play a part in its failure due to my lack of fulfillment. I was all over the place chasing the next awesome object. I kept looking out instead of within.

I heard spiritual leaders, pastors, and mentors tell me that I had to be content. To find contentment wherever I was. It didn't matter the situation, I could still find contentment in the midst of it. I began praying and working on being content. I had some success, but it was not consistent so I became more frustrated. Again, I began to give up on my dreams and my desire to do something great. I gave up on my real purpose. I began to think that something was just completely wrong with me and I couldn't be "fixed." At one point I thought God was mad at me for all the things I did in my past and that this was my punishment.

When my wife left, I finally hit an awareness I had never experienced before. I saw things about me that I did not see before. They were things I repressed down either because of shame, or to eliminate the pain I was feeling at the time. As I began moving forward and working on myself, a domino effect began to surface in other areas that I did not realize. I realized my past was never really dealt with and that was the barrier that was holding me back from reaching my potential.

Before I sat down to write this book, I was reflecting and I had the realization I was content where I was. I was okay being alone and I had a peace that I had never felt before. For the first time in my life, I was content and happy with being alone. If you have never experienced this feeling, it is absolutely amazing. Of course there are times when I get lonely or frustrated. That is human nature, but it doesn't last long. I spent a year and a half healing myself, letting go of my past, forgiving myself, and becoming a better dad and person that it allowed me to get to this new place of understanding. Again, contentment does not mean complacency. I know I have to continue to grow and change, but I am (at least for the moment) content with where I am.

At the moment I realized I was pleased with where I was, my purpose began to resurface, my passion began to reignite and I found clarity! I was introduced to people that would serve to guide me closer and closer to my purpose. People that hold me accountable, that think the way I think, and push me to reach my goals. My energy and excitement began to grow and continues to grow. Opportunities began to present themselves to me almost as if by magic. It is because I am happy, I know who I am, and I focus on what I want and not what I don't want. I began to finally see the path God was guiding me on. It was satisfying, humbling, and joyful all at the same time.

Had I not gone through everything I had gone through, I wouldn't be where I am today. I wouldn't be able to write this book. Just like you wouldn't be who you are today, and where you are today, without walking through your own trials. We learn the most through our toughest times and I am so thankful for them. If I was not in a place of happiness, I could not be thankful for my hard times. It takes a different level of consciousness to be thankful for all the bad that happens to us.

I had to reach a place of fulfillment in order to achieve growth. It is absolutely amazing to see what happens when you let go and get to a place of deep peace. I never imagined I would be where I am today and being happy plays the biggest role. Exponential growth occurs once you hit a level of true happiness. Healing has to take place and continue in order to get there. Again, this is a process and it takes time. Who I am did not happen overnight and who I want to be is not going to happen overnight either. We must all grow and we can grow together.

ACTION STEPS

1. Take some time to reflect on who you are, and where you are in your life today. Are you in a place of contentment, or are you seeking fulfillment from outside? Make sure to look at all areas of your life. If the answer is seeking outside, spend some time focusing on contentment. Be ok where you are, so that you can grow to where you want to go.

2. Practice gratitude. Every morning, write down 3-5 things you are grateful for. This will set your mind in the right frame for the entire day, even if something bad arises. When you are grateful, you become content.

CHAPTER FIVE

BOASTING IN
YOUR WEAKNESSES

What does it mean to boast in your weaknesses? Does it mean to be proud of your weaknesses? In some sense yes, but it goes deeper than that. To boast in your weaknesses means to not be ashamed of them. To embrace your faults and talk about them freely without worrying about what others think. Seems so simple doesn't it? If so, then why do we struggle so much with it?

We don't talk about our weaknesses because we were taught to not show weaknesses, to hide our faults. If we let others know what is wrong with us, or what we fail at, they will think differently of us. They will judge us and turn their backs on us. They will treat us differently and walk over us. And some may, but that is okay. You don't need those people in your life anyway. The exact opposite of what we are taught is true though. Boasting in our weaknesses is a sign of strength. It lets others know that we are human and that we all have our own struggles and demons in our closets we have to deal with. No one is immune to weakness. Even the most successful people have weaknesses. Some may even have the same ones that you do.

If we want growth in our lives and to find strength in our weaknesses, we need to boast about them. As the Bible states, "In our weakness we are made stronger." It also states that, "When we bring to the light that was once in the darkness, it no longer has a hold on us." When we hold on to things and become ashamed of our shortcomings, it consumes us. We become bitter and angry, and possibly more reserved. We end up putting up a wall to keep people at a distance so they don't find out about our weaknesses. When we hold it in, not only does it affect us, but it will ultimately spill out into other areas of our lives. It can affect our relationships. It can impact our jobs, our businesses. It can impact our finances. It can consume us if we let it.

To boast in our weaknesses, we have to learn to be more vulnerable and transparent. This is not easy because it goes against everything we have been taught or have seen. When you begin to boast, you will face resistance. Your body will tense up and your mind will go crazy creating false scenarios of what might happen. Fight the resistance and push through and boast anyway. Stand tall and shout it out.

Okay, here is what I want you to do to practice standing tall and shouting it out. While you're eating dinner with friends or family, I want you to get up, stand tall, look at your plate of food and shout "GET IN MY BELLY!!!," then quietly sit back down and begin eating without saying anything else. When everyone at the table continues to stare at you, or says "What the heck was that?" Just say "What? I am passionate about good food." Okay, so this may not really help you for boasting in your weaknesses, but it sure is funny to do, and see the expressions on other people's faces. Yes, I have done this, and have even convinced others to do it as well. It is very entertaining.

Now that you laughed a little, let's talk about the science behind boasting in our weaknesses. When we boast, we break the chains that hold us back. It brings to us a freedom that we have never experienced before. Remember, we all have our weaknesses, and when we boast in them, it frees other people. It allows others to drop the baggage they have been holding on to. Maybe someone else is struggling with the exact same thing you are. How inspiring is it to watch the weight of someone else's weakness release when you speak freely? It gives them hope. It gives them courage that they, too, can stand courageously in their weaknesses. More importantly, it lets others know that they are not alone in this battle.

Although boasting about our weaknesses lets others know they are not alone, we often alienate ourselves by saying things like "no one else is struggling with this" or "no one really knows what I'm going through." We have to be more vulnerable and transparent. It allows us to be real. It allows us to be authentic. It allows us to be the person we desire to be. Boasting is actually a strength, not a sign of weakness, as I previously stated. Some people may judge you and that is okay. They have their own struggles and you don't have to deal with theirs. You just have to focus on you. That is all you can control.

Boasting in our weaknesses teach us to be humble. It reminds us of where we come from, but we do not have to be controlled by it. It reminds us to be patient and understanding of others when we get frustrated or begin to judge their weaknesses. It creates an inner peace inside of us that is indescribable. I know I have said that many times throughout these pages, but that means it's important. It frees us from the guilt and shame that weigh us down. We release it so that we can seek the life we desire. To fulfill our purpose. When we don't, we will never be able to live our lives to its fullest potential.

When you boast in your weakness you move the change process forward exponentially. What seemed like an eternity before, will be right in front of you. It will change the lives of others. It will inspire others and create peace in their lives. It will create stronger bonds and relationships you currently have. You will be able to form new relationships. People will notice something different about you (in a good way.) You will carry yourself differently. You will talk differently. You will smile differently.

By taking the difficult, yet simple step of being vulnerable, you will greatly impact all the other areas of your life. How you feel has a direct impact on what happens in your outside world. Think of hiding your weaknesses as shutting the door to the outside world and locking the door, the deadbolt, and boarding the door. You cannot get out and nothing can get in. All the great blessings in life are at the door but they cannot get in no matter how bad you want it. When you take the boards off, unlock the door and open it up, you are letting all the opportunities and blessings flow to you freely.

Do not ever be ashamed of your weakness. Take the step today and shout it out from the rooftop. With confidence let everyone know what it is. Is it anger? Is it addiction? It does not matter what it is, embrace it and step into vulnerability. You will be free and become stronger. You will be lighter. You will be at peace. You will be able to love deeper. You will be able to live fuller. You will be able to make a difference in the lives of those around you.

Up until a short while ago, I struggled with my weaknesses, particularly with anger. I hid it as well as I could, but I was consumed by it on the inside. At times it would rear its ugly head and I would lash out at others. Anger was what I grew up with and it was my main emotion. I did not like it but it was always there. I began to believe the lie that "that's just who I am," or "I'm Italian, We have bad tempers." In reality, we can choose how we act and react whether we are more predisposed to a certain trait or not. But for years, I believed I was just an angry person, and who I would always be.

I was also told that men (especially Italians) don't show emotion (except anger), and we don't show any flaws as that is a sign of weakness. After all, men are supposed to be tough and the more mysterious they are, the tougher they appear. Men are the providers and can't show any type of weakness. This was passed on to my dad who passed it on to us. I also lived with my subconscious insecurities of not being good enough and wanting to get other's approval and acceptance. All of this built up inside me and I would hide it behind humor and laughter. Until I realized! The only one I was really fooling was myself.

I no longer wanted to hold on to any of these weaknesses, but every time I tried to let them go, I failed. Ultimately everything led to me getting angry at some point. In my depression and anxiety days, this was very prevalent. I hurt many people and lost relationships as a result of my failure. My weaknesses consumed me. After I conquered my depression and thought I dealt with my weaknesses, they would later resurface with a vengeance. No matter how hard I tried, I would ultimately fail.

I would always tell myself that I would not turn out like my dad. I would be a better father. I would be a better person period. But I failed many times. I believed I picked up some of that trait from my dad. After all, I was exposed to it over and over and over again growing up. I could be happy one moment, but unhappy the next. I would speak my mind and not care if I offended that person. I was fun, and loved to laugh and have fun, but that was just a ploy to hide the pain inside. I wanted to make others happy and laugh because I didn't want them to feel the pain I was feeling. I still want to make people laugh and happy, but the purpose is different.

I finally stopped believing the lie that this was just who I was and nothing could change. I knew there was something more for me. I would show some improvement, but then fail. I would do it again, and then fail again. I wanted to give up many times, but I wanted a better life for myself and my kids, especially my youngest who needed me.

I went to seminar after seminar. I read book after book. I gathered everything I could to improve myself. I saw some results, but I still had something holding me back. I refused to share all of my shortcomings. I had to get past them by myself. I didn't need anyone's help. I'm a man! We get past things on our own. All that egotistical thinking did was made me weaker.

Since I was holding on to that egotistical thinking, I wanted to control every aspect of my life. I wanted things a certain way to create certainty in my life. Too much uncertainty made me anxious which would bring out the anger. Consciously, I knew I couldn't control everything, but deep down I was trying to anyway. I could not figure out how to transform and recondition my subconscious.

When my wife died, I had to overcome a lot and thankful that God helped see me through the darkest time of my life. I wouldn't have made it without Him. I had to do everything for my daughter and often failed. Some days I was happy and funny, and others I was miserable and angry. You never knew which one you were going to get and it wasn't fair to myself or my daughter. A lot of it had to do with what was passed on from my dad despite consciously not wanting to, and some was subconsciously from me wanting to create certainty and control.

I started doing much better, and then I entered into my last marriage. Things started off great, but then quickly crumbled. When we split, my eyes were finally opened to all my inadequacies, and I reached a place where I had enough. Meeting with a mentor of mine (who also happened to be a pastor), I shared my innermost pain and fears and that I did not want to live this way. I wanted to finally break the chains that had plagued me for years, but felt trapped. I felt all this inner turmoil pulling me in many directions with no way out.

He shared with me a scripture in 2 Corinthians 12 where Paul talked about his struggles and how God said, "My grace is sufficient for you, for my power is made perfect in weakness." At that moment, Paul realized that by boasting in his weakness, he would be made strong.

I tried for so long to do it on my own and I often failed. I was tired of it and determined to get past it. I didn't want my daughter to respect me out of fear, I wanted her to respect me out of love. I knew I couldn't do it on my own anymore. I needed something greater than me to help me. So I thought about that scripture and decided to give it a try. I was scared and nervous because it went completely against what I knew for years, but I also knew that what I had been doing was not working out for me.

I decided to share my weaknesses with others and in men's groups. What I thought the responses were going to be were completely different than the actual responses. I was certain that they were going to judge me, look down on me, and think I was a horrible person and cast me out. To my amazement, people were understanding and inspired.

I realized that we all have our own struggles that we are battling and when we share them with others, they feel encouraged. They no longer feel alone. They are inspired to keep fighting to overcome their struggles. Everyone has their own weaknesses they are dealing with. These people accepted my weaknesses without judgement and encouraged me. Now, it's my turn to inspire and encourage you.

Within a short period of time, I noticed a peace inside me. I did not feel as anxious as I had before. I felt lighter as if I let a very heavy suitcase go. My anger subsided and my awareness increased. When I did get anxious, I stopped and asked myself what I was trying to control. I would figure it out and let it go by reaffirming myself. If it was fear of the future, I would bring myself back to the present through positive self-talk. I was reconditioning myself and creating new mental habits in my brain. I still do this as the change process takes time. It took me years to get to where I was, it only makes sense that it would take time to change.

Through this new peace, more weaknesses arose, and even greater strengths began to surface. I was finally able to get the healing I so longed for. I began to discipline my daughter out of love instead of yelling. Granted, there are moments I let my anger get the best of me, I am human, but those moments are now very rare and I am grateful. I am in more control of how I react to events. I was drawn to women who felt broken, and lost, and angry. Why? Because I felt the same way and did not fully understand this until I began healing myself. I never wanted anyone to feel the pain I did. I also realized that I never wanted to be alone. Now, I am okay being alone. I am focused on being the best me and dad I can be to Kailee right now.

Boasting in my weakness was the biggest game changer in my life. I took a step out in faith because I no longer wanted the life I was living and that step brought exponential healing and growth. I have learned so much, and continue to do so even as I write this book, all because I took that leap of faith to become a better person and a better dad. I will continue to find ways to get better. As long as we are breathing, we need to constantly evolve into the best version of ourselves that we can be. In reality, when we change, we are changing into something that was already there, just waiting for us to step into. It's like the caterpillar that changes into the beautiful butterfly. We are constantly changing into a more beautiful, more stunning, butterfly. It's a journey that will never end.

Be easy on yourself as you begin your journey. It will not happen overnight. You will fail. Pick yourself up and continue on. Affirm yourself of who you want to be. Remind yourself of why you are doing it. Your why has to be powerful. Be thankful for your weaknesses. Without them you would not be as strong as you are and you would not be able to grow. Be thankful for the mess you have gone through whether your fault or not. It has made you the person you are today. Shout your weaknesses from the rooftop and watch them disappear.

Before boasting, I used to seek out happiness from things and people. I found happiness from within and from and intimate relationship with God. I sought approval from others. I no longer need to. I let go of my past. I am no longer defined by my past. Awareness brings growth, peace, and joy.

If I can do it, I know you can!

ACTION STEPS

1. Step out in courage and boast in your weaknesses. Embrace them. If you don't feel comfortable in a group setting, reach out to someone you know and trust. Share it, and share it freely.

2. Write your "why" down. Why do you want to change? Make sure your why is powerful and specific. If it does not bring tears to your eyes when you talk, or think about it, it's not powerful enough.

3. Affirm to yourself who you want to be and who you already are. Make sure you are easy on yourself when you stumble. It's okay.

CHAPTER SIX

YOU CAN'T DO IT ALONE

With everything in life we seek to accomplish, we typically have help getting there. When we start a new job, we have the help of our peers and managers. Looking to start a new business, we seek the advice of others who have successful businesses, or higher a business coach. Anything we are trying to get better at, we seek guidance from someone who has been there. It makes sense then, to seek guidance in our darkest moments too. Guys especially struggle in this area because there is something innate in us causing us to think that we have to do it on our own. If we can't do it alone, then we are weak.

It's a common belief that if a man seeks help he is weak. This is a false perception. Woman are guilty as well, but men are more prone to fall here. It actually takes a stronger person to seek guidance and to admit they don't have the answers. When we seek the guidance from someone who can adequately help us, growth takes place.

Stop thinking that you have to do it alone, or to think you are alone in whatever struggle you are in. You are not alone. More importantly, we have a higher power that guides us on a daily basis. We just don't tend to listen to it that frequently. Have you ever had a "gut feeling" about something? Or have you been somewhere and it didn't "feel right"? Ever have an idea pop in your mind that you couldn't shake? Ever "know something was wrong" before finding out something was wrong? These are just a few of the many ways that our higher power is talking to us. That higher power is God, although some may call it the Universe, Consciousness, Infinite Wisdom or the Divine. God is real and there to guide us. Listen to Him.

By listening intently, we are learning to become in tune with God. It takes being intentional and focusing on the present. When we worry, have anxiety, or fear, or sadness, it is hard to hear God because we are either stuck in the past, or focusing on the future. God is here to guide us in many ways: to protect us from danger, to guard us against negative situations, and to realize and fulfill our purpose.

If you have ever felt that nagging feeling that you were meant for more, that is God speaking to you. You must listen to Him more and allow Him to guide you. Sometimes our gut feelings are off, but we can tell the difference when it is our own belief system talking, and when God is speaking to us. Many people have stated that God doesn't talk to them, or they do not hear Him answer their prayers or requests. If we would stop and listen a little more, we would realize that He is talking to us and there is something we need to hear.

If we seek God's guidance while we seek other people's guidance, we condense the time frames it takes to achieve the growth we desire. Of course we will have setbacks or go through valleys from time to time, but the overall growth is far greater than if we were to try it on our own. Maybe you have tried it on your own and have become frustrated because you weren't seeing the results you were expecting and quit, or at least stopped for an extended period of time.

You were created for relationships and cultivate these relationships for the greater good of all. When you seek the guidance from God and other people, you get a wonderful thing called hope. If nothing else, you get hope. Hope that you can make it. Hope that change is possible. Hope that you can walk through whatever it is you are going through. When you have hope, you have everything!

You also get strength. Strength to keep moving forward when you want to quit because it is too much to bear. Strength to find the positive in the worst situations. Strength to keep fighting when you don't have any energy to. At your lowest, is when God comes in and picks you up and carries you through. You get courage knowing that other people are cheering you on and have been where you are currently. They believe in you when you don't believe in yourself.

Seeking others and God helps build character and vision. It helps you see ideas and concepts that you may not have seen yourself. They can see a different picture than you can, because they are looking in from the outside. Seeking mentors allows you to grow much faster than you otherwise would. It is wise to seek others who have been where you are currently or have knowledge of something you don't, for it will help you move forward.

Break away from the chains that make you believe you are weak if you admit you have a problem. By holding it in and trying to do it yourself, not only will you most likely fail, but it becomes a lonely dark place that consumes you and will slowly eat away at your peace and happiness. Admit whatever you need help in and you will feel a peace well up inside. An almost sigh of relief knowing that you are not alone and that others are there to help and have been exactly where you are, and that we have a God that can far exceed any human expectation possible.

When we increase our awareness and consciousness, we hear God more and are able to make more rational decisions. It takes being in the present moment to hear from God and to understand the message being sent.

There is nothing wrong with you for seeking out help. We all need help and anyone that looks down on you for seeking help is wrong themselves and has no business being in your life. It takes a courageous person to say I need help and then follow through without shame to discover the life they were created for. If you want a new beginning, you must ask for help. If you want to stay where you are or have little growth, continue doing it on your own. I hope you choose to seek God and others while on your journey. It will give you the peace and hope that you deserve and make the journey a little easier to bear.

Prior to knowing God and seeking outside guidance, I believed that you had to get through things on your own. I believed that you could only depend on yourself and no one else to get anything done. You kept your problems to yourself because if you let anyone know you were weak, they would look down on you, judge you, or take advantage of you. You solved everything on your own, and if you couldn't figure it out, you kept going until you did. You never asked for help. That meant you were weak. The only emotion you showed (other than happiness) was when you were mad. You always had to prove you were right at the expense of everything else. You didn't work through things, you just kept quiet and repressed them.

Every time I struggled with something, I would get angry but I always refused to take anyone's help. If I did, they pretty much forced it on me because I had too much pride. When I struggled with depression it took everything I had to seek help in the beginning and talk about it. Most of the time I would put my game face on. I kept everything inside and just smiled and had fun. It would build up and then I would crack. I would release it through anger mainly because that is all I knew. I would distract my built up emotions by releasing it through other means. I took up bodybuilding. Most of it was to feel better and look better, but some was to release the stress, sadness, and the consuming overwhelm from holding on to the past. Past hurts, past regrets, and past failures. All the shame and guilt I was holding on to. Working out helped me feel more relaxed but I was still depressed and had severe anxiety. I talked to a therapist for a while and was on medicine but all the medicine did was mask the symptoms.

It took everything I had to say something to my dad after all those years about how it hurt when he didn't show up at my high school graduation. It was against everything I knew, but I was tired of how I felt and knew I had to change something.

I got so sick and tired of how I felt and hurting others that I said enough was enough. I was not going to let it beat me. Over a period of a year I was off my medicine and was doing better, or so I thought. I made some changes but they weren't permanent. Because I never fully dealt with my underlying issues it would come back to haunt me. At first it seemed so subtle with lack of fulfillment. I would jump to the next amazing opportunity, because it would bring me more money or happiness. I lost motivation for a while but regained the drive to move again. I then, got my college degree and thought that would make me happy because it was a great accomplishment.

I began to unconsciously control every aspect of my life. Everything had to be just the way I wanted. And when something did not go my way, I would freak out. By controlling, I would create certainty in my life. As illogical as that seems, that is what was going on unconsciously. I would get severe anxiety, anger, and fear. My situations controlled me instead of me being in control of myself.

I was so desperate to break free from this debilitating plague that I began reading self-help books, listening to audio, and attending seminars. I would see some improvement, but not enough. I was still struggling on the inside. I acted like I was happy and content, but my actions showed otherwise. I would go on a roller coaster of emotions and that would dictate my successes and failures in life. Instead of looking inward, I would blame the failure on it not being the right vehicle, or that it didn't work. They worked for many others, but not for me.

After my wife died, I began really focusing on positive change and growth, but was still holding on to some of my old ways, like continuing to control all aspects of my life. I would ask God for help and sometimes I would get it and others I wouldn't, so it seemed. I was still looking outward at other things and other people. I was preaching positive teachings but wasn't sold 100% myself. I was not being consistent with what I knew to be true, although I knew it all worked because I used it before and got results.

I wanted change in my life so bad that I finally realized I needed help. I somewhat let go of my pride and sought mentors and coaches. People that had what I wanted or had the knowledge that I was seeking. I Sought successful business people, pastors, and other spiritual mentors. I had some growth but I still held on to some pride and control. I would give God control then take it back. I thought I was giving him control but in reality I was holding back. Old habits can be hard to kill off, but I was determined.

Realize, our hardest and darkest moments are where we learn the most. It is where we grow the most. We are usually not aware when we are going through it because the pain is real. We are in the middle of it all and it is difficult to see. We are allowing the situation to control us. Now of course I realize that there is a real emotion involved when bad things happen. It's natural and it is impossible to stay positive 100% of the time, although I used to believe that was the case. But what I am saying is that when bad things happen we need to deal with the reality of emotion and the situation, accept it, and design a plan to move forward. However, do not let it consume you or hold on to you for a long time. Do not let it consume you and control you permanently where bitterness, anger, shame, guilt, and resentment set in.

Shift your mindset from a "why me", to a mindset of gratitude and learning possibility. When you do that, you grow. That finally happened to me. I had many growing opportunities, but still had some shame I was not dealing with. The shame was coming out as anger, and I wanted to deal with it once and for all. I could not do it by myself. I sought out others. I boasted about my weaknesses. I forgave myself and others. I let go and let God. I let go of the past. I started living more in the present. I reached a higher awareness of my emotions and thoughts and began taking them captive and shifting them from negative to positive.

With a higher awareness new weaknesses presented themselves and I was able to heal from them. I went through an exponential healing process in a short period of time. I am in a state of gratitude but I have to work hard to stay there until the new belief system is fully formed. With all the distraction life offers, we have to focus and work hard at change. I have to continue seeking growth to continue getting better. When I finally let go I was freed. When I decided I could no longer do it on my own I was freed. You can be freed as well, but you must let go.

ACTION STEPS

1. Let go of the idea that you *MUST* do it alone. Stop trying to do this journey on your own. Seek God. Seek others that can mentor and guide you. Asking for help does not make you weak. It means you are courageous.

2. Surround yourself with people that have what you want in life. If you want a successful business, surround yourself with people who have successful businesses. If you are looking to grow spiritually, surround yourself with people that will help you grow spiritually. Whatever area you are looking to grow, surround yourself with people who are doing well in that area, and learn from them.

3. Read more personal development books, or listen to personal development podcasts or audiobooks. Attend seminars in the areas you want to change. Immerse yourself completely into constantly changing, constantly growing, and consider hiring a coach.

CHAPTER SEVEN

LETTING GO OF WHAT YOU CAN'T CONTROL

When we try to control every aspect of our lives we get a false sense of security and certainty. If you noticed, I said "try." Every little thing can set us on a roller coaster ride at any given moment. Trying to get our kids to do what we want, when we want. Wanting our spouses to go along with what we believe. Our work. Our colleagues. Our business partners. Our finances. Everything. We want things to go our way. But what happens when they don't go our way? We know it is inevitable that something is going to happen that we can't control.

When the inevitable happens, how do we react when we can't control something? We get angry, hurt, bitter or shut down. Maybe you are one that always has to be right and will prove it at all costs. What if you are right though? Is it worth trying to prove it every single time? We end up losing relationships as a result in many cases and alienating ourselves.

When you try to control everything, you end up losing more control. Every time you try to grip tighter and pull everything closer to you, it actually slips further and further from your grip. The cycle continues as it slips further, you pull tighter until you eventually lose complete control which includes losing control of you. Your emotions begin to control you, instead of you controlling your emotions.

The more you focus on controlling everything, the more it negatively affects your well-being. You become tense. Your health can be affected. Your relationships will definitely be affected. Your kids will drift further from you. Your spouses will stop communicating effectively. You begin to shut people out. You begin to blame others or outside factors to justify why things are happening. You shift the focus on other people and things instead of on yourself. It becomes so habitual that you begin to believe the illusion. Believing you can control every aspect of your life is an illusion in itself. The more you become consumed by controlling every aspect, the more control it has over you. The more it changes who you are.

What happens when someone dies? Or when someone hurts you? Or when you lose your job? Or you didn't achieve a goal? Or you had a financial loss out of your control? What effect do the above examples have on you? It causes stress and anxiety. It will cause health issues. It will cause bitterness, anger, and hatred, if you allow things you can't control consume you.

What can you do when things don't go your way? If you can't control everything, how do you react? What if you reacted in a positive, loving, way, instead of in a negative manner? What if you embraced the situation, instead of fighting it? Reacting positively is where you intentionally take the offensive approach. Whereas, reacting negatively is instinctively taking the defensive approach. Which one, Positive reacting or negative reacting, do you believe moves you forward and which one do you believe moves you backwards? Intentional reacting moves you forward, instinctive reacting stunts your growth. If you are constantly reacting to your environment out of instinct, you can never move ahead.

What happens when you react to your spouse's unloving comment defensively, in an unloving manner? It hurts the relationship. What happens when you instinctively react to your kid's outburst? It will negatively impact that relationship. When you negatively react to a financial hardship it keeps you down. When you are constantly on the defense to what life throws at you, it typically causes fear, anxiety, worry, etc. None of which can positively move you in the right direction.

We naturally react instinctively to all situations. It is the way we are wired. We are human and things will get to us. Grief is a prime example. Grief will knock the crap out of you, there is no way around it. But, you *can* embrace whatever feelings you are having at the moment when it hits. Do you see the difference? Again, it's how long you let it affect you that makes the difference.

I hope you see the point. We are all prone to letting things get us so we need to be easy on ourselves. As you begin to let go of things you can't control, you become more aware and can intentionally react quicker. The more you do this the quicker you will positively react. Again, it is just like working out, the more you do it, the stronger you will become. It will get to the point where you negatively react and positively react almost simultaneously. It takes a great deal of awareness to let go and not get defensive. Gaining awareness takes time, intentionality, and work.

Seek wisdom from God as well. Seek mentors and accountability partners. Meditate. Focus on what you can control which is you and you alone. When you start to get angry, or worry, or anxiety, or whatever the emotion you are feeling, stop and ask what you are trying to control. Take your thoughts captive. Once you figure out what you are trying to control ask yourself if you can control it or not. If you can't what can you do to let it go. Work through it just like you would work through achieving a goal, a plan of action. Affirm yourself of your new goal, what you really want.

This goes for unexpected events as well. Often what happens in the present, your mind immediately wanders to what you think will happen in the future. You can't predict the future so why would you focus on something you don't know for sure and can't control. But you sure do it time and time again. I still do it to this day, but I catch it very quickly. Often times old habits will try to sneak back in when a similar situation strikes again. That is why it is important to have realistic affirmations of who you want to be and what you want to accomplish. More importantly, you need to know who you are and what your purpose and passion is.

What has God put you here for? What can be learned from this situation and how can you use it to teach others? Knowing your focus and why will keep you grounded when tough times come, and they will come! You will be tested! Old habits will attempt to sneak in. However, you can stop it and reaffirm yourself. Focus on who you are, your purpose, and your goals. By interrupting the behavior, you are bringing yourself back into the present moment. That is where life is happening right now. In the present moment. Not in the past or the future but the present. You can only plan for the future by preparing in the present. If we are not thinking in the present, we can't effectively plan for the future.

Be intentional about reacting to your spouse and kids in a loving way. Sometimes it's hard when they aren't being loving toward you, but when you react with the same unloving ways, it sure doesn't make things better. When you act in a loving way, in most cases you will get a better response from your kids and spouse. They will begin to respond in a more loving way. By acting in a loving manner it positively affects your body and mind as well.

Set healthy boundaries. What this ultimately does over time is build a stronger foundation and relationship. There may be resistance at first, but eventually, there will be more mutual respect and a bond that is very close. Everyone will be happier. Communication will become more effective. It's a win win for everyone. Again, there will be times when we all fail. That is when we immediately say sorry and ask for forgiveness and continue working at getting better.

Growth is a lifelong journey and we are ever evolving as long as we are blessed to be here. Our kids and our spouses are a blessing to us although some days it may not seem that way. When things aren't going our way we need to look within ourselves first prior to looking outside. Chances are that the reason things are bad on the outside, is because we aren't doing so good on the inside. Of course that is not always the case, but often times it may be. Sometimes bad things just happen and we have to learn to be flexible. When we let go of trying to control things we can't, and focus on our own self-control, things begin to fall into place.

It's not that chaos doesn't still exist in our lives, it's that we now have more control over ourselves and no longer react defensively to the chaos. We become proactive. We adjust and adapt to the current situation. We become more aware of ourselves and how we react, and of our outside world, and can make the many adjustments necessary to keep us on track to what's most important.

As you begin to make this positive shift, there is going to be a lot of resistance. It's going to seem like things are getting worse before they get better. Your body is designed to protect and preserve what it is used to. When you begin to change and set a new belief system for your new, healthy, experiences, your mind is going to go crazy and try to get back to the way things were. Keep moving forward. That is a great sign for great things taking place.

Remember, focusing on things you can't control robs you of the many blessings in your life. It blinds you to all the things you should be really grateful for. You can control your actions and emotions and that's it. When you stay focused on you, you gain more clarity of your life and who you really are. You will experience greater peace in all areas of your life. One area will affect other areas. By focusing on controlling yourself you will experience greater peace and growth. Let it go, let God, and let you!

Growing up with a dad who tried to control everything pretty much destined me to do the same although I said I would never be like him. Unfortunately, it was programmed into my subconscious so unless I changed the programming, I was already doomed. Add that to the other negative programming in my mind and it's no wonder I tried to control every aspect of my life.

All the negative self-talk programmed my mind so I acted accordingly whether I wanted to or not. I really believed that if I could control all areas of my life, I would be secure and ok. I knew better and would try to make changes but they were temporary. Without dealing with the deep rooted problem, I would be on the roller coaster. I would see success for a while then the old habits would creep back in again.

I wanted my kids to act a certain way, and do what I told them all the time. When they didn't, I would get mad and yell. I didn't like to get angry, but that was all I knew and it would happen when I couldn't control it. If something went wrong with my job, I would get angry and speak out. I was once told that I was honest to a fault. I had no filter and spoke my mind. If you didn't like it, too bad. Luckily I changed and react in a more compassionate way now. I now have a stronger relationship with Kailee, and my personal and professional relationships are more meaningful, and deeper.

Prior to my awakening, I didn't care how people felt or thought. I always had to be right (another trait I picked up from growing up), and would fight to prove that I was right. Even when I wasn't right, I would get madder and not admit I was wrong. When I got mad I would stay mad for a while and hold on to it. I wouldn't apologize really and if I did, it wasn't really sincere. One minute I could be happy and having fun, the next I was mad because something didn't go exactly the way I wanted.

I was miserable on the inside and I wanted to change but could never figure it out. I would try tip after tip and would have some success then fail, like I said. I began to wonder if this is just how I was going to be. After all, I'm Italian and "that's just how we are," right? The problem was, I didn't want to buy into that stigma anymore. I wanted out permanently. So I kept searching and praying.

When people hurt me I would let it consume me. I would hold grudges that would later manifest through health issues, anxiety, or increased anger toward them and others. I essentially let those that hurt me have control of my emotions. When I had financial troubles, I would freak out and worry to the point I couldn't do anything else. If I did, most of the time it wasn't a very rational decision. If the car broke down, or an unexpected bill showed up, or a host of other situations that added to my financial woes, I would lose further control which caused me to lose complete control of myself. I never had control of me, it seemed. I was defensively reactive to every situation and person including my own thoughts. I am not good enough constantly rang in my ear. I'm a failure. I'm a bad dad. I guess this is how life is going to be for me. These, and many more thoughts, ran through my head worsening my situation.

Trial after trial was strengthening me and preparing me for the ultimate change. The moment when I would finally stand up and break free from it all. The change was instantaneous, the process took time and is still taking time. When I finally told myself over and over that I can only control myself no one else did, changes began happening. When I let go of past hurts. When I boasted in my weaknesses. When I finally said this is not who I am going to be. When I stopped trying to do it on my own. When I forgave others and myself.

In that moment, change began to take place.

People will still get to me, but I do not let it keep a hold of me. Each day I am getting quicker to hold my tongue and not let myself get consumed by anger. I take my thoughts captive and talk myself through the situation and affirm that I am in control of my emotions and nothing and no one else has control over me unless I allow them to. When unexpected situations arise, I deal with them in an intentionally positive manner. I may get anxious at first, but then I quickly affirm myself and let it go.

When I feel anxious or start to get frustrated or angry, I stop and ask myself what I am trying to control that I can't. This allows me to act and diffuse the situation before I react negatively. I am able to let it go once I determine that it's not in my control and provide an alternative way to respond. If it is in my control, I figure out how to solve it. It takes time and practice just as with anything else. We are never going to be perfect while here on this earth, but we can continue to get better every day.

With my daughter, I talk with her when I am disappointed in a behavior or decision. I have found that works 100 times better than yelling. She now, respects me out of love not fear. Sometimes I have to see if it is me that is the cause of my frustration and am projecting it on her. If I am stressed or overwhelmed, it's my problem not hers. I need to check myself. I know that someday she will pick a guy like me so I ask myself often "if she were to pick someone like me today, would I be happy with the choice?" My response used to be "heck no!" Now it is "I can be alright with it but still want to grow." I will continue to grow as a person and a dad because if you are not growing you become stagnant. There is always room for improvement. ALWAYS!

Now I have more peace and can see the many blessings that are before me. When we are consumed by our past and faulty programming we miss out on so much. It affects our health, our relationships, and our spiritual well-being as well. When we can finally create lasting change then and only then can we truly live. We're not promised tomorrow so focus on the blessings of today. We can only control ourselves and that is where we need to look first before looking anywhere else. We allow situations and people to have control. When we stop and regain control, our lives are more fulfilled. It's not that bad things won't happen, or people won't hurt us, we just strengthen the control we have on ourselves and take a proactive versus reactive approach.

ACTION STEPS

1. Take the offensive and begin strengthening your awareness to how you react to all situations. Are you reacting mostly positively, or negatively? Keep a journal of your thoughts and reactions daily, so you can reflect and make adjustments.

2. Focus on what you can control which is YOU. When you start to get angry, worried, anxious, or whatever your "go-to" emotion is, stop and ask what you are trying to control. As you are practicing awareness, this will become easier and easier to do.

3. Take your thoughts captive. Once you figure out what you are trying to control, ask yourself if you can control it or not. If you can, determine what you need to do to resolve it. If you can't, let it go. Verbally say you choose to let it go.

CHAPTER EIGHT

WHAT YOU FOCUS ON GROWS

What is meant by the phrase what you focus on grows? The answer is your thoughts and what you tell yourself, as well as what the outside world exposes you to, have the greatest impact on your life. Your thoughts come from the programming in your subconscious mind which is the accumulation of everything you've experienced from growing up, from your parents, your teachers, etc., from others that have had an impact on your life in both a negative or a positive way, and from society as a whole. Much of this was programmed between the ages of 5-10 years old, so how you were raised determines, in a large part, your thoughts and outcomes.

Science and the Bible have proven that what we focus on we attract into our lives. Studies have shown that our thoughts determine our actions. Every thought we have, every word we say to ourselves, generates neuropaths in our brain. So when we want to change something in our lives it most definitely comes down to what we say to ourselves. Where our mind goes, so will we. We attract into our lives what we think about most often. We send out energy frequencies from our bodies, and attract back similar frequencies. If we are constantly focused on negative, we will get negative. If we focus on positive, we will get more positive. Now, there are circumstances that will be out of our reach that will happen in our lives no matter how we focus, but generally speaking, what we focus on will be what we get.

Let us talk about some examples. If we are always saying we are broke, we will remain broke. If we always say "why do bad things always happen to me," more often than not bad things will happen. If we say to ourselves, "I never find the right man or woman, we will continue to find the wrong person." This way of thinking and talking to ourselves can be inputted into any area of our lives. If we look at the areas of life we are struggling in, we can trace the source back to our thinking. What we think about becomes a self-fulfilling prophecy.

Remember our thoughts are the culmination of repeated programming through life experiences. Everything we say to ourselves we will come to believe. Something as innocent as "I'm so clumsy," told repeatedly, will be programmed into our minds. We will believe, and we will become it. Our minds will then look for ways to make sure it is true. How we feel can impact what we believe as well. Our emotions can be triggered without our awareness.

So if our thoughts are the result of our past programming, how do we change what we think and what we say? That is a great question! It takes being aware of our thoughts and what we say to ourselves. If we don't pay attention to our thoughts and what we say, then how can we know what to change? It takes intentional awareness and being in the present moment. Once we become aware of what we are doing we can then begin the process of lasting change. Only through changing our thoughts and what we say, will we really begin to create lasting change. If we want results in our lives, it begins with what we say to others and to ourselves.

Our thoughts create the actions we take so it makes sense that if we want to take different actions, we have to think differently. When we just take different actions, eventually the fire will burn out from the initial motivation and the old habits will take back over. We have to get to the source first, then take the action we want to have the life we desire.

Before we can change our thoughts, we have to know what we want and why we want it. Without a strong why, we will fold at the first sign of resistance. Let's be honest, you will face resistance when attempting to change your programming. It's an innate defense mechanism in the mind when something foreign is introduced. So it is important to have a strong, compelling why. Why is it important that you make the change? What is driving you to change? Why are you so passionate about this change? What will this change give you? Who is depending on you to make this change? So when it gets hard, you can focus on your why and push through.

Who do you want to become? What do you want to accomplish? What do you value most? What are your goals you wish to accomplish as you seek your new beginning? What is your purpose, your passion? These are all questions that have to be carefully considered and MUST have clear answers to. The answers to these will determine what you begin to say to yourself to transform the thoughts which will begin to form new neuropaths in the brain. This process will take time so it is important that you have several key affirmations or self-talk to help.

What are affirmations? Affirmations are a form of self-talk that you tell yourself over and over again to remind yourself and keep you focused on what you want to achieve in your life. They help you form new positive habits. Self-talk/affirmations can be created for any area you wish to change in your life. It could be a goal you want to achieve, or a belief you wish to change. Affirmations remind you of what you want so that you can take action toward that goal.

If you want to feel more worthy, tell yourself you are worthy over and over again. Go ahead. Do it now. Look at yourself in the mirror and say "I am worthy." Say this affirmation with enough feeling and eventually your brain will begin to believe it and find ways to show that you are worthy. If you want to earn X amount of money, tell yourself that you earn that much money, then design self-talk to focus your thoughts around that goal so that you believe you can earn X amount of money. The problem with most goal setting and affirmations is that the mind does not believe they can be possible because of the programming. So what we say and actually believe will conflict with each other.

If you don't change the mindset, you will begin seeking the goal only to be pulled back by the old, broken, programming. Does that mean you will achieve that goal every time? Not necessarily, but you will be further along than if you weren't and your mindset will definitely be more positive. If you continue pursuing the goal long enough, eventually you will achieve it, so don't ever give up.

Changes will not happen overnight, but over time there will be a significant noticeable difference and you will be able to achieve the goals you set out and maybe even blow them out of the water. Life is a marathon not a sprint, remember that. It all comes down to what you are telling yourself surrounding the goal. Your programming creates your beliefs which create your attitudes which create your feelings which create your actions which create your results. Be specific. Declare it. Envision it. Feel it.

We have to say the affirmations in the present tense, as if we are already living that goal. The brain does not know the difference between what is real and what is not. For example, if you do not feel worthy, your affirmation can be "I am worthy," or maybe more specific as to what you are worthy of. That way when the thought of unworthiness comes up, you can take it captive and replace it with I am worthy. The more specific the self-talk, the more specific the programming and more lasting the change will be.

Continue to tell yourself you are worthy until you firmly believe you are. Again, this will take time so be patient and easy on yourself. Say your affirmations with passion and get your body involved. There is a direct link with our mind, thoughts, and physiology. Say them out loud with power and often and feel the energy shift in your body.

If you want to take affirmations to the next level, add visualization and writing your affirmations, along with physically saying them. Visualization is taking a goal, or affirmation, and seeing it as if it were already true. For example, one of mine is "I am a confident and inspiring speaker and coach." When I visualize this, I see myself on stage talking and walking with confidence. I feel the confidence. I can see people telling me how awesome the talk was and how it helped them. Visualization is extremely powerful. Writing your affirmations is simply writing your affirmations down every day. There is a direct connection between writing and the mind. When you put visualization, writing, and saying your affirmations, the change process increases exponentially.

This is not rocket science, and it sure isn't a secret. If you want lasting change, you have to create it. It doesn't matter what the world throws at you, you can respond accordingly and on your terms. It is how you think that determines your world and your life. Your beliefs shape your world. Your thoughts are extremely powerful, and are the key to your setbacks or your successes. If this is a particularly hard area for you, spend some time focusing on your thoughts and determine some affirmations/self-talk that are specific to your needs and begin implementing them.

In my younger years being told I was "stupid" or that "I would not amount to anything" would prove to be a great obstacle for me later in life. Although I did not believe that on the surface, deep in my mind I did, and this is where the sabotage would kick in. Any time I would begin to journey out to do something great, my programming would step in and go "whoa, we don't amount to anything," and I would find a way to mess it up. Over time, I would justify, and make excuses why it didn't work out which would in turn validate the bad programming more. Since I continued this roller coaster I began to think I was not good enough which would set a new program because over time I would believe it. Combine this programming with all the other negative self-talk and it's no wonder I struggled so much despite my burning desire to break free and do something great.

I would have some success at "reprogramming" but would go right back to the old pattern. I would read self-development books that told me to do affirmations amongst a million other things that would make me successful. The problem is that I did not take much action and I wasn't consistent. I would lose desire after a while and the flame would begin to burnout. I had a why but it wasn't really strong enough. As a matter of fact, it was kind of generic. In its most basic form, my why was a general, want to be more and do more for my daughter and family. It wasn't specific enough. What was missing was what being more and doing more would provide. What would achieving those things do for me?

It didn't take me overnight to get to where I was, so it sure wasn't going to change overnight either. I had unrealistic expectations of myself and when I didn't see results fast enough, I stopped. Again, the old programming was taking over. I was frustrated with my lack of consistency and results, but instead of trying to look within, I would look elsewhere for the next opportunity. Of course I saw some change over the years but nothing significant enough.

It wasn't until I went through the last divorce, that I finally realized what was going on. I finally had enough of where my life was. Through the work in the areas discussed already in this book, I began to see so much of what was going on "behind the scenes." I began to change some things and created consistency with the new tools, like forgiveness and awareness. With the new focus, opportunities began to open up and awesome things began to happen. I began to be introduced and build relationships with the right people, like-minded people, people that would challenge me, encourage me, hold me accountable, and had what I wanted and needed.

The fact that I am writing this book is because of one of those people. It would not have happened had I not looked within and began to get serious about changing my life. My purpose and passion grew bigger and bigger, and I resolved that I would not turn back and I would find a way. I began to implement not only affirmations, but meditation as well to help with being present and releasing the unwanted junk from the world.

Now when the old patterns come up, I am quick to stop the thought, or feeling, and reaffirming what I want and who I REALLY am, not the false perception of who I was. When I get anxious or worry, it is typically because I am thinking about the future that I can't control that stems from a past event that is not true of me now. Again, it's not always the thoughts but the emotions associated with past events that were doing the programming. When those feelings come up, the old thought patterns will begin to surface.

I am quick to counter the negative and replace it. It is a battle at times but it's worth it. This journey is no longer just about me. It's about my daughter. It's about reaching other people and helping them find their new beginning. It is way bigger than me. Your journey is way bigger than you as well. Someone out there needs you. They need your strength. They need your purpose that is unique to only you. No matter how hard it is, keep pushing through.

ACTION STEPS

1. Determine your *why*. Be specific and make sure it is powerful. Your *why* is the passion that will fuel your change.

2. Take 24-48 hours and write down your thoughts. This is to increase your awareness of where your focus is. You will visually see what the majority of your thoughts are. Are they mostly positive, or mostly negative?

3. Write affirmations to replace the negative self-talk. Write these affirmations down every morning. Say them out loud several times a day. Make sure to say them with meaning. Visualize your new goals and affirmations in the morning and in the evening before bed.

CHAPTER NINE

LIVE IN THE MOMENT

You may have heard the term "living in the moment," or "living in the present," or perhaps to just be "present." I have mentioned being in the present moment in this book. But what exactly is living in the moment, or the present, and how do you do it? These are great questions that I have even asked myself. I often wondered if it was even possible. I have been around those that claimed to be living in the present. They seemed different, happier and full of joy and energy. But just maybe they were "special" and had a certain gift that allowed them to be that way.

That special gift is inside each and every one of us. We just have to be able to tap into it. In order to live in the moment, we have to train our minds. We have to seek God's guidance. All the work we have discussed in this book helps us to do just that. We have to make a conscious effort to live each moment in the present. The more we practice, the easier it will become. At some point it will become second nature and you will live in the moment without realizing it. Life will happen that will knock us out for a moment but will be able to get back quickly.

Living in the moment is when we are not focused on the future or the past. When we worry or have anxiety we are focused on the future. What we focus on today creates the future. An experience in the past can lead to anxiety of a future event. We do not know what the future holds so why focus on something we cannot control.

The past is the past, so why focus on the past. We cannot change the past, all we can do is learn from it and grow to help us influence the present and the future. Don't take the past into the future. Just because something happened in the past, does not make it true now or tomorrow.

When we live in the present moment, we can better prepare for the future. When we are not clouded by worry and anxiety, or anger and bitterness, shame, guilt, or any host of emotions, we can make better decisions that will influence our future. Even then, the future is still unknown because we have not gotten there yet. When we worry about tomorrow and are saddened by the past, we miss out on all the blessings that are right in front of us. We miss out on the joys of today. We miss out on great opportunities. We are robbed of those moments and we will never get those back once the day is gone.

By living for today we can make a brighter future for not only ourselves, but for the world around us. We gain more peace and joy in our lives by living in the moment. Our lives are so much richer by living in the moment.

Being in the present moment affects other areas of our lives as well. It rolls over into our relationships and strengthens them. It positively influences our jobs or businesses, our finances, our spirituality. Being present affects all areas of our lives. If you noticed, all change in our outside world begins with us. It then becomes a ripple affect into our outside world. One tiny little change can make a huge impact. Being present will be that impact.

Living in the "now" not only opens our eyes to the blessings of today, it brings more gratitude into our lives. It allows us to become more aware and gain more clarity of ourselves and the world around us. It will be like you have become a new person. In reality, you have not become a new person, but a better version of the you that is already inside of you. A version that aligns you with the purpose you were put on this earth for.

Living for today will open the doors to more opportunities for exponential growth. Being present allows us to focus on what matters most to us. Our values, our priorities, our passions and desires, etc. It allows you to connect at a deeper level with God.

When we live in the present moment we stop taking things for granted and start seeing all the beauty, strength, and power that is all around us and within us. I know I am getting really spiritual here, but let's face it, whether you believe or not, there is a spiritual side to all of us. It's the reason we are connected. It's the reason we long for relationships. It's the reason we long for the meaning to life. Our personal journey to the meaning of life. We are all on a journey here that is unique to each and every one of us. The only way we find that unique purpose is by letting go of the past, stop focusing on what has not happened in the future, and live in the present. Tomorrow will be here soon enough, so focus on today.

When we are present we are more in tune with our spiritual self, with God, which allows peace, joy, love, and gratitude to enter our lives. When we are focused on today, we are more aware of our thoughts and self-defeating behaviors. Living in the moment allows us to have the best life possible while we are still here. Ever heard of the phrase "live each day as if it were your last"? What would you do if you knew today was your last day here on earth? Would you tell the ones closest to you how much you love them? Would you be sad about something in the past? Would you worry about tomorrow?

I can say with certainty that you would not be sad about yesterday, or worried about tomorrow, if today was your last day. The moral of those questions. Don't live with regret. Don't regret missing out on your kids' lives when they are little. They are only little once, so make the best of it. Don't regret *not* taking your spouse out on more dates. Don't regret *not* traveling, or whatever it is you enjoy. Don't regret *not* making positive memories with your family. Come to the end of our life living fully, loving deeper, and making an impact on the world that only you can do. Live for today!

For most of my life, I lived in the past or worried about the future because of my past. Much of it was due to my belief system from growing up. Although I thought I dealt with it, I really just repressed it or bottled it up and was not aware of it. I realized later in life that when you brush something off, or just walk away thinking the issue will go away, it will end up rearing its ugly head later. For me, it was constant struggles with jobs and happiness. I suffered from depression and anxiety for a few years. I probably suffered longer than that, but just did not recognize it. It wasn't until it got out of control that I realized that there was something wrong.

At first, I didn't understand because I would laugh and have a good time, but I later realized I was just masking what was deeper. I would often lie to myself saying that I was over something when in reality, I wasn't. I would say, "I let it go," but it would manifest later. My depression and anxiety was the result of living in the past. Depression comes from the past, often from regrets, shame, and guilt. Worry or anxiety comes from the unknown in the future and by bringing the past into the future.

Although I was faking it on the outside, I was miserable on the inside. The funny, "life of the party" Tony was a defense mechanism to hide the pain. People often told me you never knew which Tony you would get. Some days, it was the happy, funny, and awesome to be around Tony. Other days, it was the stay out of his way Tony. I hated the inconsistency, but I just did not know how to get past it permanently. I sure complained a lot though and spoke my mind. I played the victim by blaming others and outside circumstances for my current situation. I had the "I will get them before they get me" mentality.

I would later learn that I needed to change my belief system because the mind will always go back to the path of least resistance. If you recall, our thoughts control our beliefs, which control our actions. I thought if I just changed what I was doing I would get different results. But, if you don't get to the root cause, the actions won't matter. It will be like you hit a wall, but unable to figure it out. You become stuck which is agonizingly frustrating. I have seen this many times in my life, as well as the lives of others whom I have coached. They have all said, "I was doing great, but then something would always stop me from going to the next level."

What I did notice was that when things were great in my life, I was able to live in the present, but the moment storms would enter, I would lose sight of everything I learned and everything great in my life. I became a slave to my situation. I felt inadequate to provide for my family. Because I felt inadequate, I felt unworthy. Because I felt unworthy, I felt shame. Do you see how powerful negativity is? It can bring the strongest person down to their knees. I have been knocked to me knees many times. The cool thing is I got back up every time. Each time I was stronger, but the shackles were still clamped tight.

Because I felt chained down, all areas of my life suffered. My health and my family. My passion to help others. My gratitude toward others and my life. Because I lacked gratitude, I could not receive gratitude from others. If I did receive, it was not done well. It was hard for me because I did not believe I deserved it.

In our darkest moments is where we learn the most. I have said this many, many, times. Over the many dark moments I have faced, each time I was gaining more wisdom, more strength, and I was getting closer and closer to being present on a consistent basis. As with everything else, it takes time and consistency to live in the present. There will be times when life will hit you hard. How we respond determines the outcome and how quickly we move past it. I still struggle with being present from time to time, but I am quicker to get back to the moment than I used to. I am more aware of who I am, my thoughts, and what I want in life. I am crystal clear on what I want now. I have a strong why/passion. A strong why is very important because it's not if things will get tough, it's when. Your passion will determine if you can push through or not.

Even in the present moment, chaos can be swarming all around you. Choose to respond in a positive fashion, instead of in a negative fashion. That is the difference. Everything happens for a reason, and each moment is designed to help you grow, to prepare you for the next step toward fulfilling your purpose.

We are not promised tomorrow so why worry about tomorrow? It may never come. I used to constantly worry about the future. Because of my worry, I missed great moments with my older kids and my youngest. I was "too stressed" or angry that I would not be in the mood to play. I don't want that anymore. I want peace. I want love. I want memories from today. I want fulfillment. I want meaning. I want purpose. I want passion. I can only fully have all of these by living today. Because I live more often in the present than I do the future or past, I am at more peace. I am able to love fully. I am able to make more of a difference with absolute passion.

When I start to stress, I immediately bring it back to the present and work on finding a solution if I can. If not, I say okay, what can I control? Me. So I need to control my feelings and my actions. Because I live more in the moment, I am more aware of my surroundings and soak in the blessings and am more grateful for everything in my life. I am even to a point that I am grateful for all the extremely trying events that have happened in my life. That kind of gratitude can only come when we are living in the present moment. Come join me in the present and watch a dramatic shift take place in your life. You are not promised tomorrow so live for today. Love deeper today. Live more fully today. Make a difference today.

ACTION STEPS

1. Take an honest assessment of your current situation. Do you live with worry, anxiety, or depression? If you answered yes, begin intentionally focusing your mind on today only. If you are writing in your gratitude journal we discussed in your action steps for Chapter 7, this will be a great start. Stay consistent every morning writing in that journal.

2. Be intentional about setting weekly date nights with your spouse (or significant other). How you treat your spouse, is how your sons learn to treat a woman and how your daughters should be treated by men.

3. Be intentional about spending uninterrupted time with your kids. Take your daughters out on dates. Take your sons out to do what *they* want to do.

CHAPTER TEN

WALKING THROUGH GRIEF

Grief affects everyone differently. The process is similar but the way in which someone walks through the process is unique to them. There are five stages of grief: denial, anger, bargaining, depression, and acceptance. Not everyone goes through all the stages and how someone goes through the stages may differ as well. There is not a process of first there is this stage, then this stage is next. A person can skip stages, go back stages, or any mixture of them. Some people grieve longer than others, and others never seem to escape grieving.

Although it is very tough and at times feels almost impossible, anyone can walk through grief successfully and become a stronger person. As a matter of fact, going through grief will change you in many ways. You will become more passionate. You will become more compassionate. You will be able to love on a deeper level. You can empathize fully with others who are going through grief in whatever capacity it may be. If you are reading this chapter and have recently lost a spouse, or loved one, and are currently grieving, I want you to know there is hope. You will make it I promise. How do I know? Because I have been through it.

I know firsthand that horrible feeling and pain of grief. It hurts deeply to the point you wish it was a horrific nightmare and you are going to wake up and reality will set back in. But you wake up and the nightmare begins all over again. There are days when you just want to sleep to escape the reality of your situation. There are days when you cannot move, think, and barely function. If you have kids that is the only reason you do function. The pain is so deep you can't even explain it to someone. You want it to go away but it doesn't. It can't go away. You have to walk through it.

You have to go through "the firsts" of everything. First anniversary without your spouse. First holidays. First birthdays. First event for your children. First mother's day or father's day. First day of school. The one year anniversary of the death. The firsts are the hardest and this is where you will go back and forth through the grief stages. There will be days when you feel ok and others when you just fall apart. You have to learn to adjust to the "new reality." How someone adjusts involves many different factors and is different for everyone.

There is no guideline on how long someone should spend grieving although there are many "experts" out there that believe there is, or try to tell you it's time to get over it and move on. That couldn't be further from the truth. Take however much time that is needed to grieve. It does not matter if it is much shorter or longer than the average person. In all actuality, you never really fully stop grieving the person. What really happens is you get to a place of healing where you can move forward. You will always love that person and will always miss that person, but you are able to move forward and it gets easier. Anniversaries of the death will always stir some emotion and memories no matter how long it has been.

When walking through grief you have to learn to take each moment at a time. Whatever emotion you are feeling, feel it. Don't fight it or you will just make matters worse. Let it come and be present with the feeling. If you are sad and crying uncontrollably, then cry. If you are angry, be angry. If you are happy, be happy. In the beginning, you may have to take it one second at a time, or one minute at a time. As the days go on, it will be a moment at a time.

If you have kids, you may be jealous of your friends who are married and have kids. You may be out in a public setting and see families together and get angry. You may be out somewhere and constantly be reminded of your loved one and breakdown and cry. It is ok. It is absolutely ok to feel these feelings. Whatever feeling you are feeling, let it be. Do not fight it. You will notice that when you let it be, you will be able to get through it a little easier. Notice I did not say easy. It won't be easy but it will be easier. If you need to lay around all day and eat chocolate, or whatever it is you crave, then do it. Stay in your pajamas all day and lie around. Be one with your emotions.

Connect with someone that has gone through what you are going through. Just knowing that someone has been where you are, is comforting and provides hope. This is a very critical time in your life and hope is really the only thing that gets you through. The pain is so unbearable in the beginning and hope eases that pain. Plus, when we know others know, it is somewhat of a relief.

If you have kids, lean on your kids. You will find they will be your rock, and you will be theirs. Pray and lean on God heavy. He will carry you through. If you get angry at God, that is ok too. He is a big boy and can handle it. Just don't turn so far away that you lose sight of the truth. God is not punishing you for something you did wrong. It is an unfortunate event that happened but it is not anything you did wrong. Find a pastor, spiritual mentor, or another leader you can turn to that will walk with you. That will guide you and tell you what you need to hear not what you want to hear. Someone that will love on you but will speak the truth to you out of love.

This is a very vulnerable time and many things can influence you. You need to surround yourself with the right people that will guide you. Attend grief groups in your area if you feel comfortable doing so. Lean on a strong family support group if you have one.

Go out and have fun. It's okay to have fun even though at times you may feel guilty. If you have a moment of happiness, embrace it. As the days go by, you will have more of these days. Don't be ashamed to smile or laugh. Laughter is part of the healing process so embrace these moments as well.

Don't let grief consume you to the point that it destroys you. Destroys who you are, your health, and relationships. Don't allow yourself to become bitter. Let it out and reach out to others. Don't bottle it up and shut down. Someone in this world needs you and you are still here for a purpose. In time that purpose will be revealed. Someone is looking up to you.

Take your time figuring things out and adjusting to the new normal as I call it. Again, there is no time frame for how long it takes you to adjust to your new normal. Each person's journey is different and how they walk through it is unique to them. Some may adjust quicker than others and that is ok. This is not a game, and you do not have to compare yourself to others. And do not listen to others who have no idea what you are going through, who try to tell you what you should and should not do. Grief is tough but you can make it through. You will make it through and be a better version of you.

Losing someone is the hardest thing you can go through, although grief does not just happen with death. It happens with divorce, losing a baby or finding out you can't have a baby, losing connection with a spouse, and grieving our pasts. But death is the hardest thing I have experienced, especially with it being unexpected. I still remember that night my wife died five years ago as of the writing of this book. I can recall every little detail of what took place. Trauma engraves the pain deep into your mind and heart and can be relived vividly if allowed to. Unfortunately, some people stay here and that alone consumes them. I don't go into the great details because I don't want to relive that night.

I am now going to shift gears and explain in greater detail, the stages of grief and how I walked through them, so that it gives you a foundation if you are walking through grief, or ever have to. Again, there is no linear way of walking through the stages. It isn't first there is denial. Second there is anger. Third there is depression. And so on, and so on. You may go from one stage to another, and back again. Some stages, you may never go through.

The first stage is DENIAL. This is where you deny that the loss actually happened. You may think, or say, things like "this is just a bad dream and I am going to wake up and everything will be back to the way it was." Even though you know that is not true, you will still think it.

For me, I felt like it wasn't really happening. The next few days after her death, definitely felt like a dream for me as I prepared for the funeral and tried to make sense of it all. I kept thinking that I was going to wake up and Jen was going to walk through the door with her smile and perky energy. Even after the funeral I still felt this way. I was numb for weeks afterwards and just went through the motions of the day.

I am so thankful that I had my daughter, family, and friends to lean on. I later found that my little girl would be my rock along with God. I would go to sleep and would dread waking up the next day because of the pain of reality. Everything was there of hers that reminded me of her. It looked as if she was still there, but I knew she wasn't. The pain was so unbearable at times that I did not know how I was going to make it through the day.

As with all the stages, don't try to push off the denial of losing the person you love. Don't tell yourself that you are "stupid," or "foolish," for believing they will come back. It's grief, and it's a powerful force. Accept it.

The second stage is ANGER. In this stage, you will get mad at the person who died, yourself, and even God. You will get mad out in public when you see families (if your spouse passed and you have kids), or even be jealous of your friends, as I mentioned. This is normal and there is nothing wrong with you.

I went back and forth with the anger stage. I went from denial, to anger, to depression, back to anger. I got mad at Jen for leaving me, and leaving me to raise Kailee by myself. If I went somewhere, or did something that reminded me of her, I would break down. When I would go to the zoo or somewhere public, I would get angry when I saw families together. I would often think, or say, "this is not fair, why do they have a family and we don't?" "My daughter should have her mommy." I got jealous of friends who were married and had kids. I got mad at God many times as well. "Why did he do this to me? Why am I being punished?" These questions, and many others, went through my head.

Many days I felt regret, which made me angry with myself. I often asked, "Why didn't I check on her again sooner?" That regret plagued me often until one day I finally realized (thanks to a great mentor) that there was nothing I could have done and to stop blaming myself.

The point to remember here, is that it is okay to get angry. It is okay to get angry at God. Just don't turn your back completely on God. That is a very dark place to be. Embrace the anger, it's part of the process, as counterintuitive as it may seem.

The third stage is BARGAINING. This is where you bargain with God to bring the loved one back. It is the last remaining remnants of hope. If they have died, you plead with God to bring them back. If you are recently divorced, you are asking for the marriage to be brought back together. If you recently lost a baby, or found out you can't have a baby, you are pleading to have the outcome, or results, reversed.

This is the stage where you say, "God, if you just bring them back, I will do this." The "this" is whatever you are willing to do, or give up, in exchange for getting back what you lost. It could be that you will go to church every weekend. It could be that you will change the way you behave, or the actions that you take. It could be that you are will-ing to give up something in return. You are begging God to reverse what has happened, and are willing to do "anything," in return. Bar-gaining is similar to a sense of denial. You are denying the reality of the situation and wishing things were back to the way they were.

I went through this stage briefly, then immediately went into the depression stage. When I was performing CPR on my wife, I was praying for God to perform a miracle to let her start breathing again. Even when the paramedics showed up and they used the paddles to shock her heart, I was hoping, even though I knew she was gone. I did not want to come to grips with reality. After paramedics pronounced her dead, and I had to tell my daughter that her mommy died and went to Heaven, is when I shifted from bargaining to depression.

The fourth stage is DEPRESSION. Depression can be a feeling of overwhelming sadness, or it can be something deeper where you fully feel the loneliness and emptiness of every day. This feeling is deeper than you can ever imagine. Unless you have gone through it, you can't fully understand it, because the pain you feel is so indescribable.

In this stage, I got extremely scared, especially in the beginning. If you recall, in my earlier years I suffered from depression. I did not want to go back to that place. But this experience was a million times more difficult. I was at a fork in the road with one way leading to bitterness and destruction to me and everything around me, and the other lean-ing on God and asking for strength. Thankfully I chose the second one! I never got depressed per say, other than the normal associated with the grief. I never went back down the hard road I once traveled.

Of course I was deeply saddened and cried. In the beginning, my emotions were all over the place. One minute I was "okay," and the next I was crying. I often wondered what the heck was wrong with me. I would try to fight it, but that just made things worse. I eventually learned to be present with my emotions.

The fifth and final stage of grief is ACCEPTANCE. Acceptance doesn't mean that you are okay with the loss of your loved one. It just means that you have come to grips with the physical reality that your loved one is gone and not coming back. You will never be okay that they are gone, you just learn to move forward a day at a time.

My acceptance came around the six-month anniversary of Jen's death. It was around this time that the days got a little easier and more bearable. My sadness wasn't as frequent and I was able to do more. I was able to laugh more and not be ashamed of laughing. The sadness and memories do not ever go away though, as I stated before. I still miss her and always will. The timeframe for entering the acceptance phase is different for everyone. Some will take longer than others. You cannot force this stage. It comes naturally.

Now that I have discussed each stage individually, and briefly how I walked through each, I want to continue walking you through the process as a whole. I can't mention enough that you will not go from one step to the next. Imagine it as if you are on a wave in the ocean. Just like the tides flow in and back out, you too, will flow in and out of the stages.

I flowed back and forth several times through the anger and depression stages. Recall back in the anger stage when I asked God why He was punishing me. I took those same questions and asked them to my mentor when we often met after the death. I still remember his response. "Why not you, Tony? He has a greater purpose for you here and he will use this to do great things through you. Although I don't know what it is, he will reveal it in time and when you're ready." He then said, "I don't know what you are truly feeling, but I do know this, God can make good out of bad, because God is good." I responded angrily with "how the hell can he make good out of my wife dying, he can't bring her back?!" My mentor responded with "I don't know, but God will reveal it to you when you're ready." Years later I now understand the good that is coming out of it. The whole reason this book is here is because of that situation. It led me on a path of exponential growth that will now be used to help many others, possibly around the world. And so my purpose was born!

Prior to knowing my purpose, some days were absolutely horrible and all "the firsts" were crushing. I would be fine and then I wasn't. I would laugh and then cry. Sometimes I would even feel guilty for laughing or having a moment of happiness. Grief can play some tricks on you. Its okay to laugh and its okay to cry, and it's okay to get angry or jealous. It is part of the process. What is not okay is holding on to the emotions and the pain. I had to let it out. I had to show my daughter that it was okay to talk and share emotions. Some days I had to be strong for her. Other days I had to show her I was weak. She was my rock, and I was hers. She is still my rock. She teaches me so much now and I am so grateful that she is in my life and God chose me to be her daddy.

I learned to go with the emotions I was feeling and become flexible with the emotional roller coaster. If I was happy, I embraced it. If I was crying, I embraced it. If I was angry and bitter, I embraced it. If I was at a ballgame and started crying because of memories of us going to games, I embraced it. I was not ashamed one bit. If I had to lay around all day because I just was not strong enough to do anything, then that is what I did. Embracing the emotions allowed walking through them to be so much easier. The emotions would fade quicker and I would feel better faster than when I fought them.

I remember a few times where people told me it was time to move on, that it had been long enough. At first, I wanted to yell and punch them. I thought to myself "how dare you to tell me to get over it." I realized they meant well. It was a case of wrong use of words and bad timing. That and the fact they did not experience what I was going through. Unless you have been through it, you have no idea what it feels like, so you have no right to say "get over it" to someone else. Even if you have gone through it, everyone experiences it differently, so you cannot truly understand what they are feeling. When you are ready, you will move past it, although there is a natural process if you move with it instead of against it.

Now I am more compassionate and empathetic to others who are going through it. When a few close people I know experienced similar tragedies I actually cried because I remembered the pain, and knew they were experiencing that excruciating pain themselves. I joke around and say I am a big baby now because I can tear up at certain situations even on TV. But I'm glad I am the way I am now because I can relate and help others on a deeper level. It has changed me into the person I am today. A better version of me that will continue to evolve and overcome. I can connect on a higher level with other people, whereas before I was unable to. I have learned to be vulnerable. Vulnerability is courage in disguise.

ACTION STEPS

1. Take each moment at a time. Whatever emotion you are feeling, feel it. Don't fight your emotions. Fighting will only make matters worse. Embrace the feelings. If you are angry, be angry. If you are sad, be sad. If you are happy, be happy. If you feel like crying, cry.

2. Connect with someone that has gone through what you are going through. Just knowing that someone has been where you are, is comforting and provides hope. Connect with a pastor, mentor, or leader that you can be open and real with, someone that will love on you but speak the truth to you out of love.

3. If you have kids, lean on your kids. They will be your rock, and you will be theirs. Pray and lean on God heavily. He will carry you through. Even if you are angry with God, lean on Him.

FINAL THOUGHTS

I want to thank you for joining me on this journey and I truly hope that it has been helpful to you in your journey. I hope it has inspired you to keep moving forward even in the midst of your darkest moments. If you are in a dark place, I hope this has inspired you to see the light.

I hope you have found hope. Hope that you can have a new beginning in life because you absolutely can. It does not matter what you have done, or where you have been, or what anyone says or thinks about you. It takes a definite decision that you want a new life. A life you desire. A life you were created for. To find the purpose that is unique to you in this world. You do have a purpose and if you haven't found it yet, that is ok. Keep seeking it and it will be revealed to you. Don't ever give up no matter how hard life gets. You may get knocked down many, many times, but don't let life keep you down. Keep getting back up no matter how hard it gets, or how long it takes. It will be worth it.

I believe in you! Yes, I truly believe in you. I do not have to have met you to believe in you. If you are reading this book, then you are a person that wants more and deserves more and I believe in you. Do not compare yourself to anyone else that is further ahead of you. You don't know their story and your journey is unique to you. Embrace your unique journey.

There is someone somewhere in this world that needs you and needs you to find your new beginning. Your purpose needs to be shared with the world so keep fighting. I know you can do it! Let this be part of your why!

I love you all and take care! Connect with me and let me know how your journey is going and how I can further help you along the way.

Your Friend and Coach,

ABOUT THE AUTHOR

nthony "Tony" Fonte is a New Beginnings coach, author, speaker, and most importantly a dad. Inspired by the tragic loss of his wife in 2011 and the many life experiences he walked through, Tony began a journey of intense personal growth and vulnerability where he learned tools to help him create a new beginning for he and his daughter. He was, and still is, intentional about overcoming a tragedy and his past so he can be the man, and dad, he wants to be. Now he teaches these same tools to help others achieve their new beginning and transform their lives and relationships. You can feel, and hear, the passion when Tony works with clients either one-on-one, a group setting, or from the stage. The systems and tools Tony uses help others achieve results extraordinarily fast. He believes that life is a journey, not a sprint, and hopes that New Beginnings will help you enjoy the ride.

Meet Tony and receive several free resources at
www.tonyfonte.com

LOOKING FOR A SPEAKER
THAT WILL NOT ONLY INSPIRE,
BUT WILL CREATE LASTING CHANGE?

Would you like Tony to speak at your next group or event? Simply go to tonyfonte.com/speaking and use the contact form. Tell us about your event and we will work together to create a perfect program for your audience.

Current Programs Include:

1. *Vulnerability:* Courage in Disguise

2. *The Abundant Life:* 4 Keys to Creating Happiness that Lasts

3. *The Resilient Mind:* 4 Habits to Weather Any Storm

4. *Walking Through Grief:* Learning How to Survive Loss and Rediscovering YOU

www.ingramcontent.com/pod-product-compliance
Lightning Source LLC
Chambersburg PA
CBHW020918090426
42736CB00008B/689